A journal of nature & story

Get in touch

info@elementumjournal.com

Elementum Journal

81 Cheap Street, Sherborne, Dorset

DT9 3BA, United Kingdom

Connect

Twitter @elementumjournl

Instagram @elementumjournal

Facebook @elementumjournal

Buy or subscribe online

www.elementumjournal.com/shop

Become a stockist

If you would like to stock

Elementum, please contact

trade@elementumjournal.com

Cover image

Alaria esculenta by Anna Atkins

As Kingfishers Catch Fire

Images from *As Kingfishers Catch Fire,* copyright Alex Preston. Reprinted with permission from Little, Brown Group. Printed in the UK, 2017. Images copyright Neil Gower.

Anna Atkins – Cyanotypes

From the New York Public Library.

Emma Turner

Images from *Broadland Birds* (Country Life, 1924), *Birdwatching on Scolt Head* (Country Life, 1924) and *Stray Leaves from Nature's Notebook* (Country Life, 1929).

Wild Amateurs

Grateful thanks to Charlie and Will at Timber Millers, Sherborne, Dorset.

To those who have shaped us the most, thank you.

ISBN 978-0-9956740-2-8 ISSN 2398-6301
A CIP record for this book is available from the British Library.
Elementum Journal is a biannual publication.

Printed in the UK on FSC certified and Carbon Balanced Paper. The impact of the print production of *Elementum Journal* has been compensated for, or balanced, by the World Land Trust – an international conservation charity.

SHAPE

EDITION FOUR

ELEMENTUM

CONTRIBUTORS

WRITERS & EDITORS

Jane Atkinson
Hazel Bird
Tim Birkhead
Whitney Brown
Will Burns
Rebecca Clark
Neil Gower
Jane Lovell
Susannah Marriott
Kym Martindale
Wyl Menmuir
Jackie Morris
James Parry
Alex Preston
Helen Scales
Alex Woodcock
Annie Worsley

PHOTOGRAPHERS & ARTISTS

Anna Atkins
Georgie Bennett
Rebecca Clark
Lucy Eldridge
Tor Falcon
Neil Gower
Catherine Hyde
Jackie Morris
Peter Smith
Lys Stevens
Emma L. Turner

CREATIVE & MARKETING

Rachel Blackmore
Gemma Broom
Gill Crew
Mike Hayes
Sam McArthur
Leigh Peregrine

EDITORIAL & CREATIVE DIRECTION

Jay Armstrong

FOREWORD

During the final stages of producing this edition, it became apparent that the amount of content exceeded the space available, meaning there was a real possibility that I would need to cut a number of features. Having worked alongside the contributors for many months, I felt protective of their work. Each piece – holding its own magic and telling a unique story – was quite different from anything I'd seen before in print. The solution I came to – increasing the extent of the journal from 144 to 160 pages – seems simple enough but was not made lightly. *Elementum* has been growing and maturing in many ways since its inception, and it seems apt that the edition themed 'shape' takes a different form from the others.

It has been a huge privilege working on this edition – learning from expert scientists Tim Birkhead, Helen Scales and Annie Worsley, and continually being amazed by the exceptional work of acclaimed artists Neil Gower, Catherine Hyde and Jackie Morris. I'm delighted to bring to a wider readership those whose work is perhaps less well known but carries equal weight – the exquisite cut-glass prose of poet Jane Lovell, the insights of expert lacemaker Jane Atkinson, Will Burns' vivid heart-tearing verse, and the astonishing artwork of Tor Falcon and Lys Stevens. Complementing the illustrations of two young millennials, Georgie Bennett and Lucy Eldridge, comes work from two extraordinary women born in markedly different eras – the botanist Anna Atkins (1799–1871) and the photographer Emma L. Turner (1867–1940).

Writing in the preface to her book *Broadland Birds*, published in 1924, Turner began:

> *This is not a book for the scientist nor the collector, but for the bird-lover, who may be either, or neither, or – such are the vagaries of human nature – all three. It does not pretend to be a textbook of ornithology, neither does it attempt to solve any of the problems of bird life.*

Similarly, I don't think *Elementum* should be considered a textbook, nor does it offer concrete solutions to the many problems threatening the environment. Perhaps *Elementum* has something in common with the likes of Turner, who continues:

> *It is enough for me that birds* ARE, *for I feel with James Lane Allen that 'birds never seem quite to belong to this world'. I am as shy of attempting to explain their actions from any mere human standpoint as I should be of interviewing an Archangel, if such a winged visitant should deign to alight on my island.*

There are many opportunities to come to a deeper appreciation of the natural world – through the meticulous research of experts and the work of those who have spent a lifetime recording and observing, or through the tales of storytellers whose medium is paint or lace, ink or graphite, stone or light. *Elementum* will continue to make room for these diverse voices from all age groups and from across the centuries – writers and artists who share the same purpose and whose hallmark is a sense of wonder.

Jay Armstrong
Editor

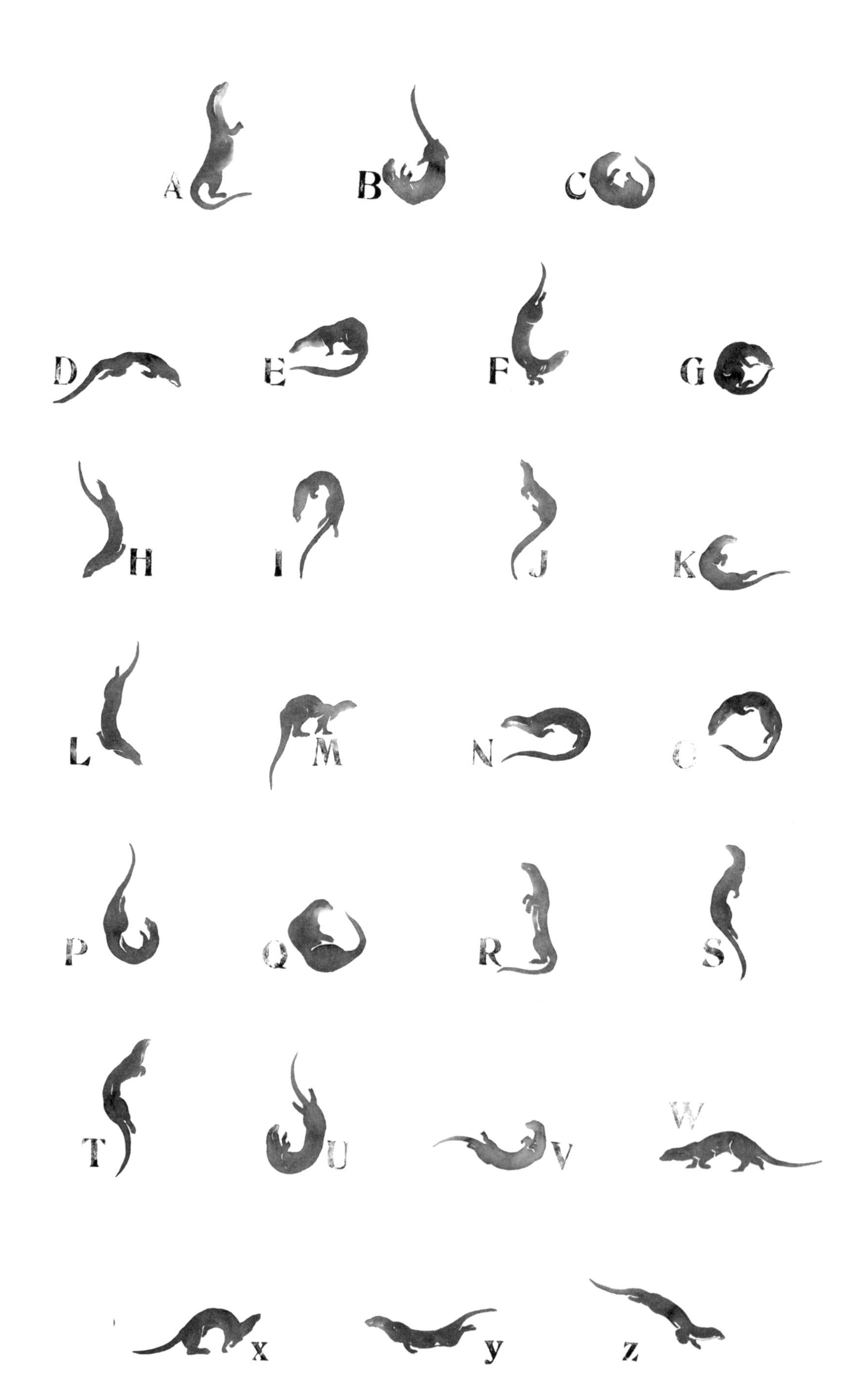
A B C
D E F G
H I J K
L M N O
P Q R S
T U V W
x y z

CONTENTS

DRAWING FISH

LIFE LINES AND FACE PRINTS

Words: Helen Scales
Illustration: Lucy Eldridge

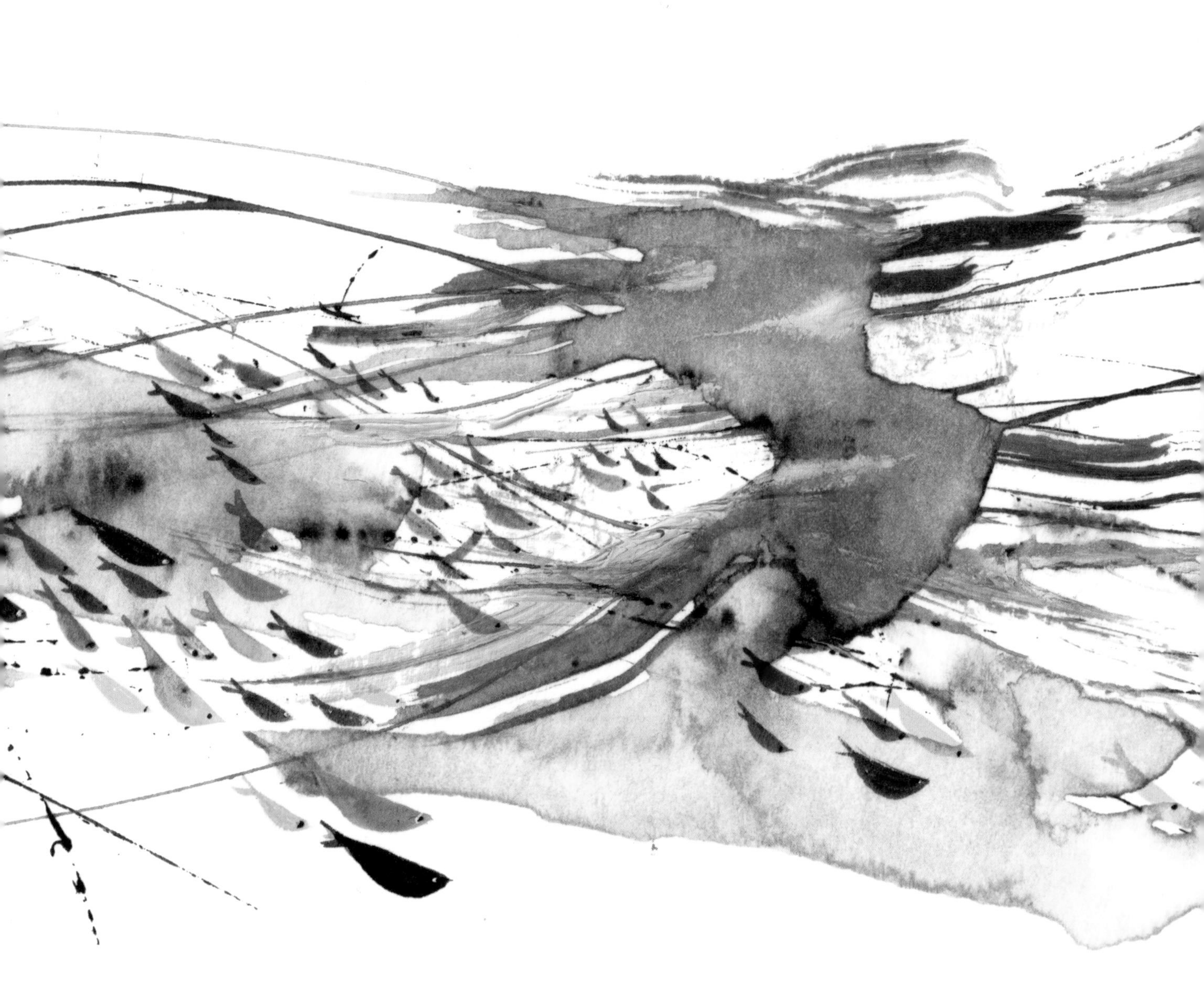

Shifting through water, fish leave ghost shapes, trails other marine creatures can read but we can only imagine. As a British marine biologist follows these threads of a fish's life, from dot on a coral reef to sweeping shoal, she uncovers ways to safeguard their survival.

Let me show you a shoal. There could be a thousand silver-blue fish here, but I confess I haven't counted them all. Each one would fit neatly on your open palm, with a shape so typically fishy it could be a child's drawing – a squashed circle for a body and a forked tail. The name of their species, if you like knowing such things, is the violet sweep or blue maomao – or *Scorpis violacea* in the official language of species naming.

For just a moment, I'll pause the shoal and hold it still (because I'm in charge here) and lower you into the midst. Now, the shoal starts up again and all around you bodies glint, as sunbeams catch scales. So many pairs of eyes turn at once to watch and hold you briefly in their gaze, checking to see that you mean no harm. Then they return to their milling; for now, these fish have nowhere in particular to go.

Now I'll change something else. The fish in our shoal begin to cast in their wake coloured, textured trails marking where they move and how they shift the water out of the way, throwing it behind themselves flick by flick to push their bodies forwards. Now, a net of tangled lines grows around you, spun into the water by the crowd of fish, which come close but never quite touch you.

What, then, if I could do this for all the fish? (It's a big ask, I know.) If they all left colourful trails reeling out behind them, what would we see? What shapes would they draw and what would we learn about their lives? How long until not a droplet of water would be left uncoloured and un-swum?

We could find a new shoal of small silvery fish, anchovies perhaps, and give each one a trail of a different colour. But, rather than muddling all of their colours together as they swam, some parts of the shoal would stay pink, others turquoise or emerald. The fish know their place. There are leaders at the front, the bravest and hungriest ones who want to get food first; the followers are content to stay further back and watch their neighbours for cues on where to move.

When danger looms near, the shoal somehow gathers its collective thoughts and becomes a coordinated school. Our lines draw closer, in tight formation. Synchrony is the key to survival so predators can't tell fish from fish.

Reaching crisis point, the school forms a tumbling sphere and our trails paint arcs of flashing colours, like running through a rainbow – violet then indigo, orange then scarlet, the colours keep changing as all of the fish try to dive into the school's middle and hide from danger. In the scrimmage, they take turns to be the outermost, exposed members of the school.

We could leave behind the whirling school of anchovies and follow instead a single fish throughout its life, drawing a solitary thread from the shoal's tangled net. Or a clownfish, perhaps, with its orange skin and white, natty stripes. It begins as a dot on a coral reef, where an egg patiently waits before it hatches and the emerging fry then drifts away into the open sea until there's only blue water and nothing to rest upon. For a time, our line shifts up and down, side to side (don't forget, we have three dimensions to play with). Here the line is drawn by a new hatchling whose fins and muscles aren't yet strong enough to resist the pull of tides and currents, which might push it for hundreds of miles. In due course our meandering line takes on more purpose. It's not a dead-straight line – that would be difficult in turbulent seas – but no doubt there's intention and a destination to reach.

So far, this line has taken days to draw, perhaps weeks, as the new clownfish makes its way to a place it hopes to call home. We follow the trail to a coral reef, likely somewhere different from where we started. There, a new pattern unfolds like a dot-to-dot puzzle, but it's hard to make out what the picture's supposed to be.

Every dot is a giant anemone, a restless mop of tentacles that already has plenty of resident clownfish and no more room, even for a small one.

At last the line reaches a final dot and here it stops. Over time it begins to loop in circles round and round the anemone and up into the water – the clownfish does his bit to shoo intruders away, but always he comes back to tentacles and safety.

For years and decades the line continues in tight scribbles, rooted to its anemone, until eventually – if ours is one of the lucky clownfish – new lines begin to be cast outwards, into the blue.

We've been following a male, as all clownfish are to begin with. He has to wait his turn while all the older, bigger, stronger males hog the queen's attention and tend to her eggs. As soon as one male dies, the next in line takes his place, biding his time. And, if he stays alive long enough, he'll eventually experience anemone life in a whole new way. One day the female will die and the biggest male will take her place, spontaneously switching roles and changing sex. When this happens, he will stop making sperm and start making eggs, becoming the lady of the anemone.

Of course, the fish don't need me to make up these coloured lines for them. They've already figured this out for themselves. They have their own ways of knowing.

Underwater creatures leave ghosts of themselves behind, marks in the water that can hover there for long minutes before smearing and drifting away. Us humans can't make out these ghosts but to fish, with their tingling sixth sense, the water is full of them. Most fish have deep, jelly-filled pores on their snout connected to networks of tubes beneath their skin that detect and deliver precise details about moving water molecules. What feels like a gentle, nondescript swish of water against our skin is, for a fish, a fin-print rich with information. It tells them another fish was here. Or a shrimp (they feel the water patterns left by the shrimp's many fidgeting legs). Or a hermit crab dragging its second-hand home, encrusted with sponges and wormy tubes.

We'll probably never grasp what it feels like for a fish to know who passed by lately, what neurons fire and what memories are sparked by those quivering tubes of jelly, what pictures they see in their mind's eye. But they know it was a parrotfish sculling past with dips of its pectoral fins. They recognise the nervous flit of a small damselfish, darting to its hiding place. They know whether there's a fish to avoid – an ambush predator with its stop-start wide paddle of a tail, sloshing water to the sides, or a hunting eel drawing snaking lines. Or it could be a fish to chase, slow enough to catch up with, small enough to swallow.

For us to know where the fish go, we must make up other ways. We can haul a fish from the water, clip on a coloured tag and a note, then let it go again like a message in a bottle, hoping someone somewhere will find that fish again. Then we'll know two things – where the fish started and where it stopped; everything in between we can only imagine.

There are much smarter tags these days that report back on the fish's position all along the way, helped by radio receivers and satellites and computers with maps. There goes a youthful bluefin tuna, racing from Japan to California and back again to do all the things it needs to do – eat, breed and eat some more. There dives a devil ray, flapping its wings through deep layers of microscopic food.

If enough fish congregate, we can fire sheets of sound into the water and listen carefully for the echoes (we've built machines to make the sounds and do the listening for us, then tell us what they've heard). Pictures made from bouncing sounds show the gathering together of millions of herring into heaving, sweeping shoals many miles across.

Simpler but more laborious methods can track fish throughout their long lives. To learn where they began, we can hunt for their eggs and young larvae, such as floating leaf-like baby eels, adrift in the Sargasso Sea. Even if we can't actually see the fish on the move, we can make good guesses about where they go by tracking currents and tides. And, after they've died, we can extract the stony bones from inside their ears and measure chemical messages left by the waters they swam through as youngsters and old, wise fish.

Once, I spent months watching fish. I peered at their faces and saw patterns I hoped would tell some of their secrets – things no one knew but them.

Golden twisted stripes drew labyrinths on their cheeks, over their sharp-sloping snouts and across their bee-stung lips. Dots and lines, loops and circles, all flashing bright against the jade greens and electric blues of their skin. Backwards from their eyes were three lines, like black kohl drawn with a shaking hand. One of their many names, the Māori wrasse, tells of those patterns that perhaps look like the designs inked onto the faces of New Zealand warriors.

These were the patterns I watched and photographed, day after day. I came to see them at one special spot on a small coral atoll surrounded by hundreds of square miles of open sea. This spot was where the wrasse came at certain times, when the moon was full and the tides tugged sharply at the reef's water.

Māori wrasse are of a grander stature than most fish on a reef, beaten only in size by sea turtles and cruising, long-distance sharks. They normally live alone, wandering by themselves unconcerned by the needs of a partner or the strict rules for following others in a shoal. But, when the time comes to find a mate, they all know where to go and what to do.

At the spawning site, where I waited for them with my camera, most of the giant fish were females. A few old timers were males – one was in charge, and the rest hoped to be up on their luck when his back was turned. The daily event lasted several hours as females paraded in twos and threes, pursued by the eager male. And they took turns to join him in the water above the reef to release precious clouds of eggs to meet and fuse with his sperm.

The purpose of my study, and my growing obsession with those patterns on the faces of the wrasse, was to learn how to spot who was who at the spawning congregation. I wanted to know whether the females who showed up at this site were new ones each day, delivering their single clutch of eggs and then returning to their solitary lives. Or were they the same fish coming back many times, a small group working hard and making clutch after clutch, between them sharing the responsibility of releasing all those new, tiny fish into the world? To know that, I needed to learn the patterns on each face and show, as I hoped, that they were unique to each fish, like a fingerprint. A fish's face print, I suppose. And so, with hundreds of photos of fish in focus, and thousands thrown away that were no use, I began to see the same faces. There they were, day after day, mating over and over.

Ultimately, I uncovered these patterns in the fish's sex lives so I could write a thesis and get permission to call myself doctor (Helen Scales, Doctor of Fish, you've got to admit, has a certain ring to it). But I also had other, more selfless ideas in mind. I imagined that the answers to my questions might hold sway in the difficult, colliding worlds of fishing and conservation, livelihoods and profiteering.

The Māori wrasse is right near the top of the list of ocean species that could be hunted to extinction. If we're not careful, they could blink out. Their endangerment stems from demand for their tender flesh in expensive restaurants across Asia, in China especially. Diners peer into cramped aquarium tanks at colourful fish and decide which they want to be taken away and cooked; the lips of the biggest males are said to be a delicacy. To supply this demand, fishing fleets pursue these species and take every last one they can find.

My quest, then, was to find out just how vulnerable the Māori wrasse are when they gather together to mate. Are these spots on the reef crucial places to protect? As a scientist, I knew I had to report my results as I found them and not lean towards the answer I wanted. But, deep down, I felt compelled to show how much these spawning fish matter and how they need to be watched and looked after. And indeed, that's what I found. I showed that it wouldn't take much effort for fishermen to come along, find these places where the wrasse spawn and take them all away. Once the females are lost, there won't be more coming along to fill their place. It's not rocket science – fish out the fish, and then they're gone. But just how swiftly they could vanish is a shock and a warning.

There are other ways my findings can be used. Should you want to know how many of these huge fish there are in a population, there's no need to swim around and find each one so as to conduct a head count across the reef – just find the place where they spawn, if you can, and wait for them to come to you. Don't catch them – just watch them. Count all the fish at the spawning site, preferably over a few days to reassure yourself that this is how things really are, and there you have it – a fish figure, to compare and track changes over time.

I didn't get to do that, though. A little while after my first visit to this spot, I heard that all the wrasse, the ones I'd learned to recognise and come to think of as 'my fish', had been lost from the reef, just as I'd warned myself. They'd been taken away by one of the roving fishing fleets that chase after these big fish and send them off to be sold for the highest prices.

It left me hollow, knowing what had happened to all those fish. All the while as I'd been focusing in on the details of their lives, there had been wider forces at work that would ultimately matter far more than any of my findings.

In time I've come to a more hopeful outlook on the oceans and everything that lives there. I had to, really, or give up entirely on studying and writing, talking and caring about it all. There are still Māori wrasse out there, and each time I see one (which isn't often) it reminds me that it's not too late – there's still so much to protect and cherish. And sometimes I let myself wonder whether some of those young wrasse escaped and survived, the ones I watched being made. If they had drawn lines through the sea, I could have followed their paths. Maybe some lines would have reached a faraway reef where these fish are now taking turns to throw their own lines of new life out into the blue.

STORIES IN THE SANDS OF TIME

IMPRESSIONS OF ANCESTORS

Words: Annie Worsley
Artist: Lys Stevens

LYS STEVENS

Even the greatest mountains eventually come to rest in the sea, reduced over deep time to silt and grains of sand. There, within the smallest fragments, are libraries of lost stories and memories of peoples long gone. On a beach at Wester Ross in the Scottish Highlands, footprints hint at those tales.

North and west from the great rock pinnacles of the Scottish Highlands is a land of wrinkled coasts defined by its geology, far-reaching vistas and the westering sun. Sculpted by ice, wind and water, crafted by soils and vegetation, and moulded by the histories of its people, this is a place of champagne light and velvet dark, orchestral sound and glacial quiet, swirling eddies and patient stillness. Wester Ross is a part of this west-facing world and, along with the islands of the Outer Hebrides, is made from some of Earth's oldest rocks. Stored within their crystals and minerals are fragments of the planet's most ancient stories; I have always felt a curious sense of alignment to them, and to the seas and sunsets of the west.

I farm on a croft that stands at the edge of Wester Ross atop a low cliff where the views are exceptional and expansive. I have followed a long and winding trail to this place from my red-brick birthplace in industrial North West England, via the sandy coastlines of Merseyside and Lancashire where I raised a family and worked in academia as a physical geographer.

The croft is a smallholding of peaty riverside ground that has been farmed for generations. Ancient paths and tracks branch out from the fields, some east towards the hills, others west towards the sea, in a network resembling a spider's web. Over countless years, wild creatures as well as humans have created these routes – many are almost invisible beneath tunnels of twisted heather and curling grass, while others are broad, long and well-used stony bridleways. And in this landscape veneered with history it is not hard to imagine

layers of footprints, compressed and invisible, each set of feet with their different purposes and particular meanings, as ghost lines, whose weight, configuration and orientation are mysterious and coded, yet even now able to exert influence on the ground they cross.

Now the path I take daily from house to wildness bears the marks of my passing. It runs across the croft meadows, along a stony track with deep grooves made by feet, hooves and carts, to an old wooden kissing gate. Its latch is long gone, its hinges are orange with rust and its wooden laths are patched with grey-green crustose lichen. A frayed blue length of rope is used to keep the gate closed to sheep and winds. This is now a doorway to another place, and every time I cross the threshold I feel a little wilder.

From here a narrow trail, little more than trampled turf, sheep-feet wide, heads to the cliff edge. Curling, it then strikes down towards the shore. The cliff is not a rocky precipice; it is covered with clumps of heather, grass and myrtle, and large multicoloured cushions of moss. Water seeps out through the turf and from small exposures of peat and stony soil that are sheep scrapes. It is a radiant and variegated steep slope that copes well with the salt and grit flung skywards by fractious autumn winds and winter storms. Mossy mounds defy the textbook descriptions of where they are commonly found: *Sphagnum* on flat bogland, *Polytrichum* in old forests. Here, they cope with salinity, cold, exposure and steep gradients by growing in deep, thick pillows the colour of red wine, jade or flax.

At the foot of the slope the path turns north to run along the shore. It is bordered on one side by the tumbled rocks and shingle beach of Fiadhair Mor, then wanders through rich grassland to a rocky outcrop known as Fiadhair Beag, and finally travels on to the sandy shore of Gaineamh an Openham. The sands are dusky rose and, in some places, patterned with red ochre swirls. But pick up a handful of sand, look closely and the complex geologies of Wester Ross are there in miniature: sandstones of every hue from pale beige to russet, dusky pearl limestones, glistening quartz, and the hornblendes, biotites and feldspars of Lewisian gneiss, glowing in viridescent green, cinereous grey and rich chestnut.

Below the tiny hamlet of Opinan, this small peach-red bay occupies a hollow carved out by ice thousands of years ago. Less than half a mile long at low water, it is backed by a sand-dune system and dune grassland known as machair, which is rich with flowers in both spring and summer. Sediments, eroded from the high mountains for millennia and carried seawards by countless rivers and burns, eventually form sub-marine rolling sandbanks. They, in turn, are driven onshore by prevailing westerly winds, sluicing tides and waves to create the curved sandy bay and the deep triangle of sand dunes typical of Wester Ross. Sand comes and goes; often whole swathes of beach vanish in a single tide, depending on wind and wave direction. Occasionally storm winds and tidal eddies scrape the beach away to reveal the underlying rocks and boulders of moraines deposited some 12,000 years ago as ice sheets and glaciers melted. But they are soon covered up again. Sand grains, shells and seaweeds settle and are then dragged along by water or bounced by winds. They form ripples, ridges and runnels, and pile up on the leeward side of stones and debris, eventually forming great sloping banks of sand once more.

This aeolian, sandy place is an artist's workbench, filled with beautiful artefacts, paints and tools of the trade. A new work is created with every tide, though many disappear unseen as night-waves wash away a line of shells here, a bracelet of bladder wrack there, a ghostly remnant of foam here, a heaped raggle of shining stones there. The tide knits and knots seaweeds, weaving it with strands and tangles of coloured ropes, while shells, crab carapaces and feathers are spread out in collages, occasionally decorated with bones, old shoes, bottles and branches from distant lands.

Often, after a spell of stormy weather, the sea retains some atmospheric energy and large, slow-moving waves continue to break gently and calmly along the shore. As they sweep in, they push tiny pieces of shell and seaweed before them; as they retreat, the almost microscopic fragments are left sitting millimetres proud of the smooth beach surface. What is left is a line made in the likeness of the wave. Each one leaves its own new mark and together they create a series of interlocking shapes. Within a short space of time the sea draws silhouettes and profiles, shapes and shadows akin to the pen-and-ink mountain landscapes painted by the Chinese artists of the Song dynasty.

Such delicate artistry, by a sea whose storm waves can rip apart fences and walls and topple cliffs, is enchanting. Each line of sand-landscape, a faint yet well-defined impression of the wave that drew it, is a ghost story, a tale of lost geographies. These sea-drawings could be manifestations of other worlds, or landscapes from a remote past. Perhaps the sand grains, eroded fragments of the very rocks that make up this wild country, have retained land-shape memories, imprints of mountain and valley topographies of which they were once a part, aeons ago.

Or perhaps this is sea-art, oceanic photographic memory. In the same way we once kept films and negatives, these fragmented remains of long-since-eroded lands, lost to the oceans yet retained within them, are delivered onshore to be redrawn by the whimsy of wave motion, in a thalassic treatise, a salty photo album. The sea might even hold the most ancient memories of Archaean earth: through minuscule fragments of Lewisian gneiss come images of Hadean landscapes; using grains of Torridonian sandstone, the deserts of the pre-Cambrian era; and from slivers of angular brecciated conglomerates, ice-age glacial valleys.

The little beach is also a busy place. Footprints are superimposed on the wave paintings, and my own trails in the sands criss-cross with those of birds and animals and occasionally insect feet. Braid-lines of three-toed footprints reveal the determination of oyster catchers, bar-tailed godwits, curlews, gulls, dunlin, turnstones and ringed plovers feeding ahead of a rising tide. Cloven imprints of deer, cattle and sheep purposefully cross the sands in search of salt on rocks and piles of kelp, while the dig sites of dogs at play are randomly strewn.

But it is otters and their footprints that bring me the greatest joy. Their trails shadow a lively burn that cuts through the dunes. In contrast to the pale green-greys of marram grass, its narrow gully glows with bright green fringes of flag iris and other freshwater-loving species. And, because the water can change from a trickle to a torrent, it provides a small but complex habitat favoured by animals, birds and insects. This is also a route for dragonflies and sand martins, whose helical flights mirror the sinuous rippling of otters as they pass from sea to holt.

And so my footprints merge with otter spoor and the meandering spiked tracks of feeding birds. Often, depending on the timing and height of tides, our commingling trails will still be visible the following morning, dishevelled impressions collapsing inwards as sand grains trickle down into the hollows. Eventually, just as the wave art is washed away, so our footprints disappear as they too are gathered in by the sea.

Some years ago I wandered the great sandy shores of the Lancashire and Merseyside coast in search of other lost landscapes. In contrast to Opinan, there great flat sheets of ochre and peach sands spread out for miles, and from time to time the sea seems to vanish in the west. In places sandbanks overlie estuarine muds and other deposits, filled with evidence of the past. Decades of scientific study have revealed how this coast has changed over time, as the sea level has risen and fallen, rivers have come and gone, and dune systems have expanded and retreated. Most fascinating of all are the solidified muds and silts that contain human and animal footprints.

Some of these footprint-bearing sediments were exposed by wave action near the small coastal town of Formby around thirty years ago. With the fascinating serendipity that occasionally accompanies scientific research, between 2001 and 2008 I worked with a gentle man of letters called Gordon Roberts. He had been carefully recording, photographing and cataloguing the hundreds of animal, bird and human footprints that had begun to slowly emerge from the sands. For a short but very happy time, we gathered evidence of the print-makers and of the environments in which they had walked some five to six thousand years ago, he through his meticulous record keeping and measuring, I by searching in the sediments for microscopic evidence of landscape history in the form of spores, pollen and fragments of charcoal.

The footprints often occurred in trails. Gordon's extensive records have enabled specialists in anatomy and physiology to differentiate between male and female, adult and child, and individuals who walked or were running. There are long-striding hunters – in some cases, males more than six feet in height – hunting with dogs, and poignant impressions from an adult female whose straight path was encircled again and again by the small feet of at least three children. There are no other records of the lives of these coastal people. Only their foot-shapes remain as ghostly archives of a very different world, captured on warm days at low tide, when the sun was shining and their prey – animals or plants – was abundant. As they walked or ran or skipped along, their feet sank into fine-grained muds. Warmed by the sun and in all likelihood a gentle sea breeze, the surfaces began to dry out and slowly bake. Returning tidal waters, loaded with new sediment, then filled in the imprints incrementally, and they disappeared. During the intervening millennia, successive tides and subsequent sand-dune building buried and compressed the deposits, hardening them and preserving the footprints. But, over the past few decades, as sea levels have begun to rise and coastal sand dunes have shifted, the baked and buried footprint-bearing muds have been exposed. They are truly ephemeral, for within days of being revealed they vanish again, carried away as the muddy archives themselves dissolve and scatter in the waves.

Many times when I was working with Gordon we would speculate on the lives of the footprint-makers, comparing our love of coastal environments with theirs and thinking about how the skills they would have possessed have been lost in time. Though some people still practise the ancient art of gathering marsh samphire (*Salicornia europaea*), many other hunter-gatherer methods have been forgotten, the abundances of life in salt marshes and mudflats unremembered. As we worked out how the ancient prints had been preserved, we would take off our boots and wiggle our toes in the sands and muds to leave our own spoor and in doing so enjoy our tentative connection to those ancient communities and wilder places and times. We rummaged with our feet, feeling the seeping coldness of the sediments but basking in the warmth of our shared companionship and history, for we were coastal people too, wind-blown and ephemeral.

The sand grains of Formby are derived from much younger geologies than those of Wester Ross and are different in character from those of Opinan, yet the sensation of fluctuating timelessness in both sandy places is acute. Over the years I have come to realise that, despite these land formations' intrinsically shifting nature, my roots are fixed in mobile sand systems, dunes, beaches and estuaries, like marram grass. Although the great solid rock Highland landscapes create a strong sense of place and of belonging, and mountains a powerful feeling of permanence, it is the nomadic, fluid nature of drift geologies in small bays and coves with which I have deep affinity.

I wonder whether the women of prehistoric Formby felt a similar sense of rootedness to their coastal landscapes; I feel certain they did. They carried their burdens with them – babies, pregnancy, ill-health, food supplies – and they kept their children close. And they knew the land well and were deeply intimate with it. While the most dramatic footprints tell of tall men hunting red deer and aurochs, it is perhaps the smaller, quieter actions of the women that are most moving and important. Theirs are the stories of home and hearth, of nurture as well as nature, and of understanding the deeper intimacies of space and place. These women were more knowledgeable than any modern coastal dweller – they themselves were aeolian, blowing in with the wind and following the tides.

I have never lived more than a couple of miles from the sea, having lived and breathed its particular and salted air since birth. Over the years, travelling inland was difficult – it felt wrong, as if some deep-seated quirk or twist in my DNA was trying to prevent me leaving the coast. When I lived in Lancashire, my innate sense of direction failed as soon as I crossed the M6 motorway. At the edge of the Pennines, any roads heading east would prompt a gravity-pulling flip-over in my stomach. My geo-colleagues laughed but I would simply say that more than normal amounts of directional magnetite must be lodged in my homing-pigeon brain. In truth it is more than minerals in the frontal cortex; it is something that wriggles and squirms in every cell – a molecular inheritance, fixed in bone, blood and muscle, all wrapped up with the great, seeping lure of the sea, a powerful directional force that overrides any tiny fragment of internal magnet.

mindful

It has been suggested that the essence of our paternal genes drives us to voyage and discovery while maternal coding creates the sense of belonging and a need for settlement and grounding. Whether that might hint at some deep, hidden truth about human nature, who can truly say, but what does feel right is that we are intrinsically, though often blindly and in some mysterious way, drawn to certain types of rock or sediment. Nan Shepherd wrote about granite in the Cairngorm mountains with more than deep affection – she expressed her love of their geology as deeply as air roams those wild plateaus and water sings in their deep ravines. Her words are redolent of a sense of belonging to the very elementals that surrounded her: air, water, light, ice and rock. And, in very different prose from that of many mountain writers, she describes how one walks *into* a mountain rather than *upon* it. Against the impression of permanence that mountains often engender, she gracefully expresses how raw nature is so mobile and changeable that the very rock itself is as alive and malleable as wind and water.

Osteoarchaeologists can read the lives of bodies buried for centuries. They can work out where a person lived and travelled by measuring the various elements contained within a skeleton. Nan Shepherd's bones would tell of a life lived on granite. Mine will reveal a journey from the sands of Lancashire to the ancient rocks of Wester Ross. Sadly, no human bones have ever been found in the Formby deposits; we only have the footprints preserved in Gordon's records and those impressions that come and go even now with the ebb and flow of tides. But I imagine the essences of those ancient hunter-gatherers are still held within the beach sediments and in the returning waves there, just as lost landscapes are held by and drawn in the sands of Opinan.

All mountains eventually come to the sea, moved by rivers and glaciers. Their grains are reworked and reduced to constituent elemental crystals and minerals until at last they are washed into estuaries and onto beaches. There they are used by waves to portray land-shapes on the sandy shores and muddy bays of the world, and perhaps gather up and record the imprints of footsteps.

Hidden in handfuls of sand, silt and mud in the transient environments of our wild and restless coasts, human histories merge with those distant times. These can be seen by anyone, if they pause to look. And maybe in the looking they will leave imprints of their own.

CWM ELAN

A VALLEY SCULPTED BY ICE AND DYNAMITE

Words: Whitney Brown
Illustration: Catherine Hyde

The construction of dams in the nineteenth century transformed a Welsh valley, forging from its abundant stone and cold water a liquid and financial link between countryside and city. A dry-stone waller revisits this place to discover what was lost, what was gained, and how nature accommodated such drastic disruption.

One rainy October day in 2009, Jack drove me north across the River Wye, which divides the old counties of Brecknockshire and Radnorshire before flowing onwards to England. Left in Newbridge – upstream – then left again in Rhayader, up a tributary. I didn't know where he was taking me. I was new to Wales in those days. This was long before I left my marks in stone, long before I fell in love. I had come to Wales to learn about dry-stone walls. In the end, as these things go, my journey would turn out to be a little more complicated than learning a new craft.

I had been in Wales about a month by then. Everything was new and fascinating – the shapes of every hill, every river and every glorious tangle of sessile oak caught my eye. Jack and I had been working hard on the restoration of a long eighteenth-century dry-stone wall that ran straight up a mountain in the Rhiangoll Valley. Stripping out the old tumbled wall, mending it anew with ancient techniques... I moved tons each day – disassembling, reassembling. Slowly, and with many smashed fingers, I was learning to build.

'I have a surprise for you today,' Jack said to me that morning. 'I'm taking you somewhere very special.'

This had better be good, I thought. It was pouring – a day better suited to hiding under blankets by the wood stove.

Mist hung in the trees. Yellow larch, evergreen spruce, rowan, beech, birch, oak. As Jack drove me deeper and deeper into this valley that Saturday morning, my jaw dropped a little lower with each bend in the road. He had told me nothing.

In a country renowned for its sublime natural beauty, this was manmade: the dams and reservoirs of Cwm Elan (the Elan Valley). Stone escarpments, flaking away with time and weather, shot up alongside the narrow road. Arched stone bridges curved elegantly across expanses of dark, deep water. The dams were not overflowing that day, and the streams were low, too, revealing the contours of rocks normally submerged – smooth, scoured monuments to the passing of time. We stopped the car and I walked the riverbed, stepping from stone to stone across scattered puddles. Spillways rose majestically in the distance, one after another, dry but for the rain, and all the better to take in the mind-boggling scale and detail of the masonry of each one.

Bundled in wool and Gore-Tex, I gazed in awe over the deeply textured face of Pen y Garreg, the middle of the dams of the Elan Valley. The stonework here is exquisite – tight, monumental, elegant, enduring. The Victorian designers had clearly gone above and beyond the essentials of mere functionality. The dams and spillways, the turreted bridges and the massive retaining walls are all far more beautiful than they have to be to do their job. Caban Coch, Garreg Ddu, Pen y Garreg and Craig Goch... even their names are elegant.

I couldn't help but wonder who built this... When? How?

I'm a bit of a construction romantic, I suppose. I love lime plaster, traditional joinery and hand-forged iron. Surrounded by artfully worked stone that first day, I lamented to myself how brutalist and utilitarian public works projects became as the twentieth century progressed. Concrete, steel, free of embellishment... It's not that those things can't be beautiful, but so often we don't ask them to be. The fifth dam of the Elan Valley Estate – Claerwen, built after the interruptions of the First and Second World Wars – is a half-hearted attempt at beauty, concrete faced with stone, and without question it lacks the magic of the four Victorian originals. Neither do the hydroelectric dams of my home state of South Carolina stir the imagination. They do not inspire me to wonder about the workmen who put them there.

I wondered about the men who came to shape the Elan Valley, same as I wondered about the men who built the old dry-stone walls I was now restoring each day at Jack's side. Sometimes we found the broken clay pieces of their tobacco pipes amongst the stone as we worked. These were small glimpses into their lives.

In 1890, the seventy square miles that would become the Birmingham Corporation's Elan Valley Estate were home to two manor houses and many more working farms. In a few short years, all of those lands and dwellings would be purchased, cleared of human inhabitants and submerged beneath the tea-coloured waters of modern reservoirs. In summer, when the water levels drop low enough, the remnants of Nantgwyllt Manor and its walled gardens re-emerge like the ghosts of a forgotten place.

The city of Birmingham grew exponentially in the nineteenth century as the Industrial Revolution reshaped the socioeconomic landscape of the English Midlands and, in time, of a distant Welsh valley. As the city's workshops, mills and factories developed, its population swelled, increasing six-fold in a century. Birmingham's rapidly expanding citizenry, many of them farm labourers from the surrounding counties and even Ireland, came to the city looking for a better way of life – a regular wage and a secure job. But city living came with different risks – shared public wells became more polluted as neighbourhoods became more and more crowded, and periodic outbreaks of typhoid and cholera ripped through the city as early as the late eighteenth century. The city's water usage doubled in the two decades leading up to 1890 and, realising that local wells and reservoirs couldn't keep up with demand, the city fathers began to look elsewhere for safe, clean water.

Surveyors for the Birmingham Corporation considered several sites within a practical distance of the city and one of these, around eighty miles west across the border into Wales, was the Afon Elan (or River Elan), a tributary of the River Wye. The Elan was fed by a generous amount of rainfall and, the surveyors fatefully concluded, its banks were narrow enough to accommodate a series of dams. The nearby River Claerwen proved suitable as well. In 1893, construction began.

The four main dams of the Elan Valley Estate were constructed between 1893 and 1904 at a cost of £6 million. Before work even began on the dams, special railroads had to be built to ship in men, materials and equipment. Eventually, the railroads would bring in a thousand tons a day of stone from Glamorgan in the south. (The local stone, a flaky shale, was not suitable for this type of construction and had to be blasted out of the way.) Steam-powered crushers and saws helped to form the raw materials into workable pieces while steam-driven cranes lifted the huge blocks of stone into place. These cranes worked on the very faces of the dams themselves, suspended from wooden gantries hundreds of feet high.

In the eleven years it took to build the four original dams, over 50,000 men came to work in the Elan Valley. An entire company village – now gone – was constructed to accommodate the legions of stone masons, quarrymen, railroad workers, engineers, surveyors, labourers and medical staff, and also their family members. It should come as no surprise that many navvies (as they were called) were injured during construction by the likes of dynamite blasts and as a result of falls, falling objects and stone-dressing accidents. The dangers of this kind of work were many, and safety equipment and regulation were minimal. It is said that the on-site hospital was never empty, and more than a hundred men lost their lives over the course of those eleven years, some drowning in the reservoirs. The dams reshaped not only the landscape but also bodies and lives.

So much of what came before – what it took to transform this valley – is invisible now, torn down as construction was completed and the thousands of people who came to build moved on to other work. They were not the first to leave this valley. I wondered, too, about the people who lost their lands to the rising waters.

I try to imagine both sides of the story. Some one hundred people lived in that valley and four hundred more worked on the farms and estates. In the nineteenth century, hardship – death, alienation, bankruptcy – put you on the road more so than adventure, and there is a sad symmetry that people moving to Birmingham eventually forced others to move from the Elan Valley. My own family were sharecroppers in the cotton fields of South Carolina, migrant labourers in the orange groves and greenhouses of Florida, and eventually migrants to the textile mills of cities. I imagine those rural people, on the move with both hope and heartache.

Landowners were compensated for their lost property, but what about the agricultural labourers who lost their jobs? The kind of people I come from – the kind with fewer resources – where did they go? What did they do? There was a workhouse just down the road in Rhayader and no doubt some wound up there.

It was not the first or the last time that this would happen in Wales, or other places in Britain. The notion of 'the public good' has seen many lands taken over and reshaped as watershed, or as military training grounds, airfields or bases. Not far away from the Elan Valley, just south of the River Wye and down on the Epynt range of hills, stories are still told about the seizure of farmland by the Ministry of Defence during the Second World War. No one lives there now, but the descendants of the farmers whose lands were seized retain grazing rights on their old property – their sheep know the sounds of the machines of war.

The debate over land use – who is entitled to it and for what reasons, and what its best use is and by whom – is an old one, and sometimes a ferocious one. Today, I trace the changes in the shape of the land and the people, for they are what fascinate me most – what was lost, what was gained and all the complexity that lies between. These were challenging, unprecedented times – cities running out of water, world wars – and unprecedented, challenging actions resulted. We debate them still.

Despite vast and sometimes devastating changes to this landscape, the area's sparse year-round population, coupled with agricultural controls that protect water quality from potentially dangerous runoff, has allowed plenty of room for flourishing biodiversity, and its levels of light pollution remain low enough at night to merit its designation as a Dark Sky Park. There are no street lights, and I've certainly never had a mobile signal there. This is part of the attraction, a place that seems removed from the rest of the world. But it has only looked this way for just over a century, and it has a daily connection, both liquid and financial, to a very busy, developed place.

The present-day Elan Valley, especially in autumn and winter, looks like a desolate place – beautiful but empty. It isn't empty, of course. It never really was. People have lived here since the Stone Age. There are still a few family farms high in the stark, windy hills, and Elan Village still has its share of children playing in the common spaces between the old stone cottages built by the Birmingham Corporation for its higher-status workers. But the bulk of the human presence in the valley comes in the form of nature-loving tourists and thrill-seeking motorbikers, who far outnumber actual residents in the warm months. Sunny weekends and bank holidays find the visitors' centre chock-a-block.

The transformation of the Elan Valley, whether tragic or heroic, nonetheless stands as a testament to the might of nineteenth-century engineering and the care with which the Victorians designed even the most utilitarian structures. The system was designed to be gravity-fed, and the seventy-three-mile-long aqueduct they engineered falls an inch per mile all the way across Powys, Herefordshire, Shropshire and Worcestershire into the Midlands. Even now, there are no pumps powering the 360 million litres that flow to Birmingham from Wales each day. The water travels at just under two miles per hour, taking a day and a half to arrive.

On that first visit, I didn't question any of this. I knew nothing of the history. I was simply taken with the beauty of it all. As much as I pondered the craftsmanship – which inherently implies physical activity and change – it felt to me as though the Elan Valley had always been this way. The dams felt natural to me somehow, something I didn't particularly question. That sounds strange, I know, but for all the change the Birmingham Corporation brought to this valley, it retains a misleading feeling of timelessness.

The natural world sometimes makes surprising and elegant accommodations for human attempts to control and shape it. Cwm Elan has rebounded and perhaps even flourished as a result of the dams, which in the end protected the land and many of its plant and animal inhabitants. Yes, there was loss, but there has also been incalculable gain. Perhaps those who deal in numbers can weigh the two against each other. I am a writer and a builder, and I deal simply in wonder.

I have been back to the Elan Valley many times now. I have been there in drought, when the reservoirs lap pitifully on the shores, and I have been there when every single dam is overflowing with misty, roaring torrents. I have picnicked there in the sunshine on grassy meadows. I have swum in remote corners of the manmade waters, sheltered from the prying eyes of the world by tree-lined banks and my own imagination. I have wandered up the hills in springtime with the mayflower still in bloom – exploring ruined farmsteads, mourning the tumbled roofs and sagging chimneys, wondering about the lives that played out here. I have spent time with the farmers and their children, and friends have taken me to waterfalls and rock pools hidden deep in the woods, told me tales of making love by starlight high above the dams in the night.

It is a place that is full of my own memories, but also of a sort of collective human memory – a landscape of memory, really, not all of which is visible or accessible... something sensed rather than seen. Stories linger here and there in the community, but mostly they take form in the imagination, and there is plenty of space for that in Mid Wales.

It was some years later in July. The sheep were on the high ground. It was the season of wild orchids, long days, perfect raspberries, noisy larks and bad tan lines, as we working folk are like to have. I was there to help restore a sheepfold that overlooked one of the reservoirs. Its walls were crumbling, a brittle sort of shale, battered by nervous sheep, itchy sheep, cold and ice. The weathered stone sometimes broke apart in our hands no matter how careful we were, and it was clear to see why it hadn't been suitable for the construction of the dams.

One wall we put back just as it was, rebuilding over the tops of orthostats (large stones set upright on edge). Another we moved entirely, connecting two other walls that didn't align but building a beautiful S-curve, which would give the farmer a better space for gathering. Sheep could be driven along its curving lengths rather than cowering in dead-end corners when frightened or simply stubborn.

Jack and I camped there in the fold one night that July. Our fire burned against the boulder of one of its walls, throwing shadows and dimming the stars for a time. It had been a searing day, but the heat left us after sunset and I sat close to the flames, shivering happily under my wet hair. I had waded into the cold, protected waters just after work, hot, exhausted and sun-dazzled, hoping to wash away the dust and the weariness of the day. We walked up into the hills afterwards, eyes searching for both ruins and wildflowers. We paused to gaze out over the scene below, resplendent in the late hour. The arches above Caban Coch looked more beautiful than they ever had before, and we had them to ourselves that dreamy evening.

Wales has always been a place where I have come in search of magic, not in the sense of faeries and the Green Man and mushrooms, but simply an encounter with the stark, pristine power of nature, guaranteed to overwhelm me and put me in my place every time. Wales has this kind of magic – the one that can shake me out of my modern worries, straighten out my ego and remind me of a particular kind of wonder found only under bright stars, in ancient woodlands, in cold water and in abundant stone. The Elan Valley, sculpted by both God and man, glaciation and dynamite, is the shape of my particular kind of magic.

The Elan Valley as it exists today testifies clearly to the human desire to harness the natural world for its own purposes, but it also shows how nature sometimes accommodates human workings in creative and fascinating ways. It is one of the few places I can think of where a distant, dense population's needs seem to coexist relatively peacefully with what nature wants. The valley's flourishing biodiversity is a positive result of what once felt like a drastic disruption. The land was changed forever. Lives were changed forever. But some margin of good has come of it. I challenge you to gaze at the wild orchids above Pen y Garreg in the golden light of sunset with a red kite circling above you and not feel the same.

The desire to keep the water clean has also kept the land clean, and that has benefitted many species, from lichen to golden plovers, from voles to hay meadow grasses. Twelve separate Sites of Special Scientific Interest exist now on the land purchased by the Birmingham Corporation, managed today by Dwr Cymru. There are cycling trails on the old railways, foot trails up through the forests, ranger talks and guided walks, stargazing gatherings, and open days that allow visitors into the inner workings of the dams themselves. The post van skirts around the edge of the Claerwen reservoir on even the foggiest and windiest of days. Farmers still raise sheep and cattle, sometimes still gathering in the autumn on horseback as in the old days. Anglers stand in the shallows. Photographers lie in wait, hoping to catch the perfect light or that one elusive species of bird. My walls still stand, and I return as often as I can to a landscape that has shaped me far more than I've shaped it.

A FRIENDSHIP BUILT OF BIRDS

THE JOURNEY OF A BOOK

Words: Alex Preston & Neil Gower
Illustration: Neil Gower

Remembering a childhood love of ornithology, a writer and illustrator coax birds from words into paint and experience points of connection through a mutual love of light, language and landscape.

ALEX

LONDON

I can't remember when I realised that I was becoming blind to birds. It was after seven, maybe eight years in London, and I was living in the northwest of the city, where the parks are brooding, unlovely places, and only in cemeteries did the grey sprawl of streets take a green breath. I used to walk in Kensal Green Cemetery as often as I could, hearing in the thin layers of birdsong a distant memory of something that was once richer, denser and more complex.

The birds I saw were green. Joyously, the occasional green woodpecker doffed his red cap to me, letting out a mad yaffle and then bouncing down towards the canal. Mostly, though, only ring-necked parakeets bullied their way into my sky. Like schools of tropical fish arrowing across the sulphurous city skyline, they blinded us to other, drabber, more familiar birds. I'd grown tired of the stories of their origins in London – released by Jimi Hendrix on Carnaby Street, or from the set of *The African Queen*. The truth was more mundane. They were escaped pets, probably from Twickenham, and, being used to the icy gusts of the Himalayas, found NW10 mild and convivial, full of meek, malleable local birds.

I grew up in a town on the south coast of England, and – in memory at least – it was wild with birds. Walking along the seafront it was impossible not to see the cormorants – Satan's birds – perched like dark crucifixes on the groynes and pier-stacks. Impossible, when I lay in bed in the morning, not to hear the gulls' raucous squabbling in the first light, the gradual build of blackbirds and song thrushes and twattling sparrows that grew to drown them out. We used to play cricket in the road on late summer evenings and, pinned firmly to that memory, and one with the wash of loss and nostalgia, is the image of a murmuration of starlings coming over, pouring up in a great flood of light and noise towards the South Downs. We'd all stop, dumbstruck as they passed over, and in the moments after felt touched by something sublimely beyond our daily lives.

In my head-down twenties, when I worked harder than people should and shammed at being an adult, I lost that special sensitivity towards birds, the knack of seeing the treecreeper against the bark or the buzzard high in the blue wash of sky. Partly the problem was one of daily routine. If you live in London – particularly as I lived at first in post-student days, in the east of town where there's scarcely a tree and nary a squirrel, and where your path takes you from flat to Tube to office to bar, stuck on repeat as life ticks by – it's easy to lose track of birds. Not to fall out of love exactly, not at first, but rather to lose the habit of seeing them.

The Cottage Book is a record of time spent in the Itchen Valley in Hampshire by my ancestor Edward Grey and his wife Dorothy. In it, Dorothy writes, 'We listened to the wren sing all morning, and over breakfast we said how good it was that we knew enough to be able to love it so much.' There's enough to live a life by in those lines, I think – that when we know something intimately, when we recognise the particular, love comes. But the formulation also works in reverse. If we lose the connection that comes with special intimacy, then soon affection leaches out of our engagement with the world. I'd stopped seeking out birds in a London whose avian palette – those parakeets aside – seemed balefully monochromatic, and so slowly I stopped loving them. I'd been collecting snippets of bird writing since my mid-teens – snippets that provided the inspiration for *As Kingfishers Catch Fire* – and you can trace that falling-out-of-love period in my notebooks. Not only did birds disappear from the skies above me but they also seemed to vanish from the books I read.

One of Edward Grey's closest friends was the naturalist W.H. Hudson. He lived in Kensington, hard up against the Gardens, and used to sleep on the roof at night so he might see the underlit bellies of migrating geese as they passed over. When he died, they consecrated a small coppice in Hyde Park to him, where there's a wonderful Epstein sculpture in his memory and dense hedges in which the birds throng and carol. I used to pass the Hudson memorial on my way across the park to work in the mornings, when I'd bicycle from Kensal Green into the West End. I started setting out early, so that I could stop, if only for a few minutes, and spend time with birds.

The goldfinch was the charmed bird of that place. Partly it was that I grew up in a world in which goldfinches had only recently remounted in numbers, and they still felt like something novel and noticeable. Hudson loved them because they reminded him of the bright finches of his South American childhood, and they returned the love, it seemed, coming to this small conspiracy of light and leaf and water to flash their dazzling wings and sing out their blithe, rising song. Those goldfinches called me back to birds, their luminous presence brightening the rest of the day.

As Kingfishers Catch Fire, then, is partly the story of a life falling in and out of love with birds. It's also the story of a friendship, one that built between me and the artist Neil Gower, a friendship built of birds ➳

ESTUARY

There must have been sunlit estuaries in my childhood, but I remember only dank, dismal mornings, low grey cloud bleeding into the land. Marram grass and gorse, tufts of heather, the slub and slither of boots on saturated earth, the pearl of drizzle on binocular lenses. My parents used to drive me out to Pagham Harbour near Chichester on Saturday mornings, and I still can't hear the sharp call of oystercatchers, the warning cry of a redshank, the heart-winnowing lament of a curlew without feeling the sky above me like a blanket, the boggy land shifting and soughing beneath. We are forged by the landscapes in which we exist, but we also choose them. I'm not sure what it said about the eight-year-old me, but these desolate, unpeopled spaces spoke deeply to me.

When Neil and I set out to create *As Kingfishers Catch Fire* together, I wanted to take him to each of the landscapes that had, as much as the birds that flew above them, been part of the magic of my childhood spent birdwatching. One of the things that birds do is to pin memory to place, and so the redshanks didn't exist independently in my mind from the estuaries whose mud they strutted upon. They weren't like the illustrations in a bird book, marooned in a sea of white – rather, they were part of the landscape, one with the wind and salt-tang of the air and the sound of their own plangent cry.

Neil and I decided to meet at Rye Harbour Nature Reserve (on the south coast), the saltflats that have come to replace Pagham in my birding life. It was a bleak February day and the wind was sweeping in from the east, launching gulls in crazy arcs above us, causing everything to quiver and sigh. There were avocets there, and little egrets, birds that would have sent me excitedly to report to my Young Ornithologists' Club meeting as a boy, but that were now commonplace. Mark Cocker, one of the UK's leading contemporary nature writers, describes this phenomenon well: the way we balance the few environmental success stories – avocets, red kites, buzzards – against the far more numerous tragedies. I knew enough not to feel too chipper at the sight of these once-rare birds. But it's hard not to be joyful at Rye. Sussex Wildlife Trust has done a superb job of stewarding this shifting, mutable wetland, and Neil and I saw the bright flash of a kingfisher, a ghosting barn owl and flocks of coruscating golden plover in the sky. It was the start of something, that day.

DOWNLAND

A few months ago, I was asked to give a talk at my old school. I set out early – it had been a frantic few weeks and I'd scarcely had time to prepare. I drove past Neil in Lewes, then above Brighton, under the brow of the Downs. I parked near the school and sat there, watching the spring sunlight moving across the grass, the chalk, the still-leafless trees. My happiest days were spent at that school, picking about amidst the old barns and knotty woods, watching swallows launch themselves down to drink over the pond, listening to barn owls on winter evenings, calling and answering in the high oaks that rose like sentries over the school. Now I sat there, three decades later, and I saw the whiteness that glowed beneath the grass, and with the chalk came a flood of memories.

I walked the Downs with my grandfather when I was a young boy. He was English as only an American can be, in tweed and a flat cap, striding up between hedgerows that were busy with birds. He'd quote poetry at me – he's a Hardy scholar – and we'd not be allowed to turn and enjoy the view until we were right at the top, when it felt as if we were moored amongst the clouds, up there with the skylarks. Then we'd turn, with the whole long reach of the coast stretched out below, and we'd whoop and laugh, astonished at the smallness of our lives, the grandness of what mere height could reveal.

Those early memories are laced through with birds, and I saw dozens of them as I drove up to the school gates. I got out and there was a chaffinch warbling somewhere off-stage, spring doing its stretching exercises. I looked up, past the school, to the broad rise of downland behind, and I recognised something. This country – this wind-blown, lark-strewn, chalk-blenched country – is now doubly special to me. Partly because it is such an intimate piece of my own personal history, but also because this is Neil's landscape, his Ravilious-painted homeland. It's why, of all the paintings that Neil did for our *Kingfishers*, it's his skylark that I have hanging above my desk at home. So deeply knitted is Neil into that vaunting, vertiginous sweep of downland that the painting is almost a self-portrait. A great bond has grown between us over the course of this book, and it's one that springs from a mutual love: of light, of landscape, of language.

As Kingfishers catch fire
How to Read Water

NEIL

Is it because I travelled here from black?

Is it the voluptuousness of their curves and declivities?

I can never decide why I feel such a visceral connection with the South Downs. I simply know that they are a long way from the coal mines and slag-heaps of my Rhondda Valley childhood. And they are, to my eye, the British landscape that most resembles a recumbent human form: a similarity that lends a respectful tenderness to my runs and hikes over their folds.

I have lived in Lewes, at the heart of these chalk hills, for eighteen years, but my awakening to them as muses began in July 2015 with a call from Alex Preston in London. I had drawn the endpapers for his latest novel and enjoyed the process immensely, not least drinking negronis with him at its launch in Florence. I had a feeling we could get along. He was reconnecting with birds and hatching a book that had been incubating in notebook form since his youth. It was to be a literary ornithology, a celebration of how writers across the ages have brought birds to vivid life on the page. Would I like to collaborate on it, to coax the birds from words into paint? From the opening paragraph of our sample chapter, 'Swallow', which swoops the reader straight up into the bedroom of a Charentais farmhouse, it became clear to me that it is impossible to capture birds in words without writing simultaneously about place. I learned that the same applies to painting them: what surrounds them, and even what stands between viewer and bird, can be as vitally descriptive as the depiction of the creature itself.

I also came to glimpse something deeper in Alex's writing. Behind the urban vignettes of starlings on his Hoxton windowsill and a grey heron on the Grand Union Canal, and, most tellingly, the description of his father taken ill at Stepney Green Tube station, I sensed an ache for something beyond London, beyond birds – a need to connect with a gentler place.

I write this passing high over a different city on a northbound train, looking down through layered bridges at white gulls on the gunmetal Tyne. I am transported back to another cold February afternoon, shortly after the contracts for the book were signed. Alex and I met at Rye Harbour Nature Reserve to watch birds and to devise a way of working. Slightly uncertain of each other and the intense new venture we were embarking upon, we convened with brand-new binoculars and our 'Curlew' chapter, as yet unillustrated. The estuary felt dead. We sat in a hide, scanning unpromising mudflats. It was unclear whether we were trying to detect birds or points of connection in our fledgling friendship. We moved on to another hide, from which we made out a herd of curlew picking over cold, mauve shallows. The flattened perspective of expensively ground glass made a lattice of their slender, dipping bills. The writing in our chapter was devoted almost exclusively to the curlew's melancholy call, and the silence of these distant birds seemed only to reinforce how little other life was to be seen or heard.

As we trudged back to the cars, we talked of our children – mine grown, Alex's still young. It felt as if we'd both expected more from the afternoon. The wide horizon offered the consolatory embers of a vast sunset. Then it happened: a slow panoply in the smoky dusk. First, at an eerie cry from one of our curlews, a marsh harrier drifted into the dark east, followed by the spectral wedge of a barn owl. Finally – and most propitiously for our newly titled collaboration – with a blue spark under a willow, the day's last ray betrayed a kingfisher. It felt like a benediction. We laughed and hugged goodbye. I drove home to sketch curlews.

Over the following months the friendship, trust and momentum between us grew. Alex drew on his vast collection of quotes and wove them into his own exquisite, evocative prose. Every fresh chapter he sent was simultaneously gift and gauntlet. With each one my interpretations grew more assured and ambitious. A lack of ornithological knowledge – something I had initially feared might compromise the paintings – proved unexpectedly beneficial. It allowed me to approach the images from precisely the angle this book required. Unencumbered by expertise, I could put my faith solely in the *words* to lead me to each bird's unique nature – that quintessence which Gerard Manley Hopkins referred to as 'inscape'. I became transfixed by the linguistic aerobatics writers had performed striving to capture this on the page:

> *The waxwings … with their lacquered quiffs, their berry-red and gorse-yellow cuffs and their woozy kohled eyes.*
>
> Alex Preston, *As Kingfishers Catch Fire*

I carried words into the Downs on long, solitary runs and let them percolate against the rhythm of my feet. It became a form of meditation. I could see the words more clearly beyond the immediate focus of running, in the same way that stars in the night sky are better discerned by gazing away from them.

It was high on Kingston Ridge, as tracing-paper squalls drifted over the English Channel, that I learned to view a piece of writing as a three-dimensional entity. I would search for its visual centre of gravity: that sweet-spot where an author's intents, conscious and subconscious, intersect. Across a giddy summer I worked absurd hours. I rose at four in the morning to wrangle goldfinches and thistles out of dawn thunder. I burned midnight oil, casting a skein of snow geese across a crimson elsewhere.

Often, running beneath larks on ridges effervescent with Ravilious light, I felt I was passing from the safekeeping of one sibilant sentinel to another. So many of the paintings seemed to crystallise in spikes of birdsong and endorphins. I would race home to distil them onto paper before the vision faded. It is clear now just how much of Sussex insinuated itself into the paintings: the larks, yes, but also the coarse corduroy fields near Firle above which our kestrel flickers, the white cliffs barely there behind the stooping peregrine and the boggy woodland near Iford gloaming our barn owl into ghostly relief.

Evocation of place in the writing played as crucial a role in leading me to each chapter's heart as the portrayal of birds. The vaulting amber crags of the *Snow Geese* painting will always echo for me with the words that inspired them:

> *Beheld the crash of icebergs and the slide of snowhills by the shooting light of the Aurora.*
>
> Thomas Hardy, *Tess of the d'Urbervilles*

Working on *As Kingfishers Catch Fire* proved more intense than either of us could have anticipated. It focused a powerful lens onto our selves, our lives and where we lived them. Alex and his family moved from North London to rural Kent during the process. In the penultimate chapter, he slides naked into the River Rother and swims, guided by a barn owl, a long way from the Grand Union Canal.

Somewhere amongst it all I lost my marriage. I now trace my way over the flanks of the Downs with even greater intimacy. I am more attuned to their moods, their weather, their breathing. I am grateful for their generosity as muses. Kindling birds from words into paint allowed me to luxuriate in the complexities of the English language and light. It provided the most vivid affirmation that these have been twin sources of inspiration and wonder all my life: two constant and stimulating companions on my 'scurochiaro' journey from Rhondda coal to Sussex chalk.

CATCHING THE SOUL OF OTTERS

THE RIPPLE AND TWINE OF MARKS ON A PAGE

Words & Illustration: Jackie Morris

The shape of water, the shape of otters, the shape of words – all of these flow.

And when you see an otter in the wild, you know you look upon a small god,
river king, river wolf, dratsie, *dwr-gi*. Otters have many names.

Even as they glide through their element, displacing the water, they are a part of it.

An otter's coat has more hairs per square inch than a human has on the whole of its head.
There was a time when otter fur was prized, a time when the pelt of
a king otter was a talisman sold to sailors, protection against drowning.
But to find an otter king first, and then kill it, that was the trick.

Watersnake, otr, eel-hunter, *dorrag how*. Their habitat is the waterlines that criss-cross, wind and twist across the landscape. Lines that flow from the mountain, spring, stream, beck and burn, river, ditch, canal and waterway. Garden ponds are their hunting grounds also, and village ponds, tarns, lochs and lakes. Dog otters are pilgrims, wanderers – over marsh and moor, tow paths, river banks, even in cities.

At land's edge and day's edge, in crepuscular light they turn and toss in the seaweed,
swim in the salt sea, search deep rock pools for spider crab and eel. They are fierce gods.

An otter sees the waterworld through whiskers, feels the moving flick of fish fast in the stream,
will snatch a kingfisher from the air, defiant of its royal name and make a small meal of its meat,
leaving only a cloak of harlequin feathers to mark where bird once ruled.

Sharp teeth tear eel flesh, small eyes glow intelligence and the muscled rudder of a tail leaves
only a ring, of bright water, to show where otter once was.

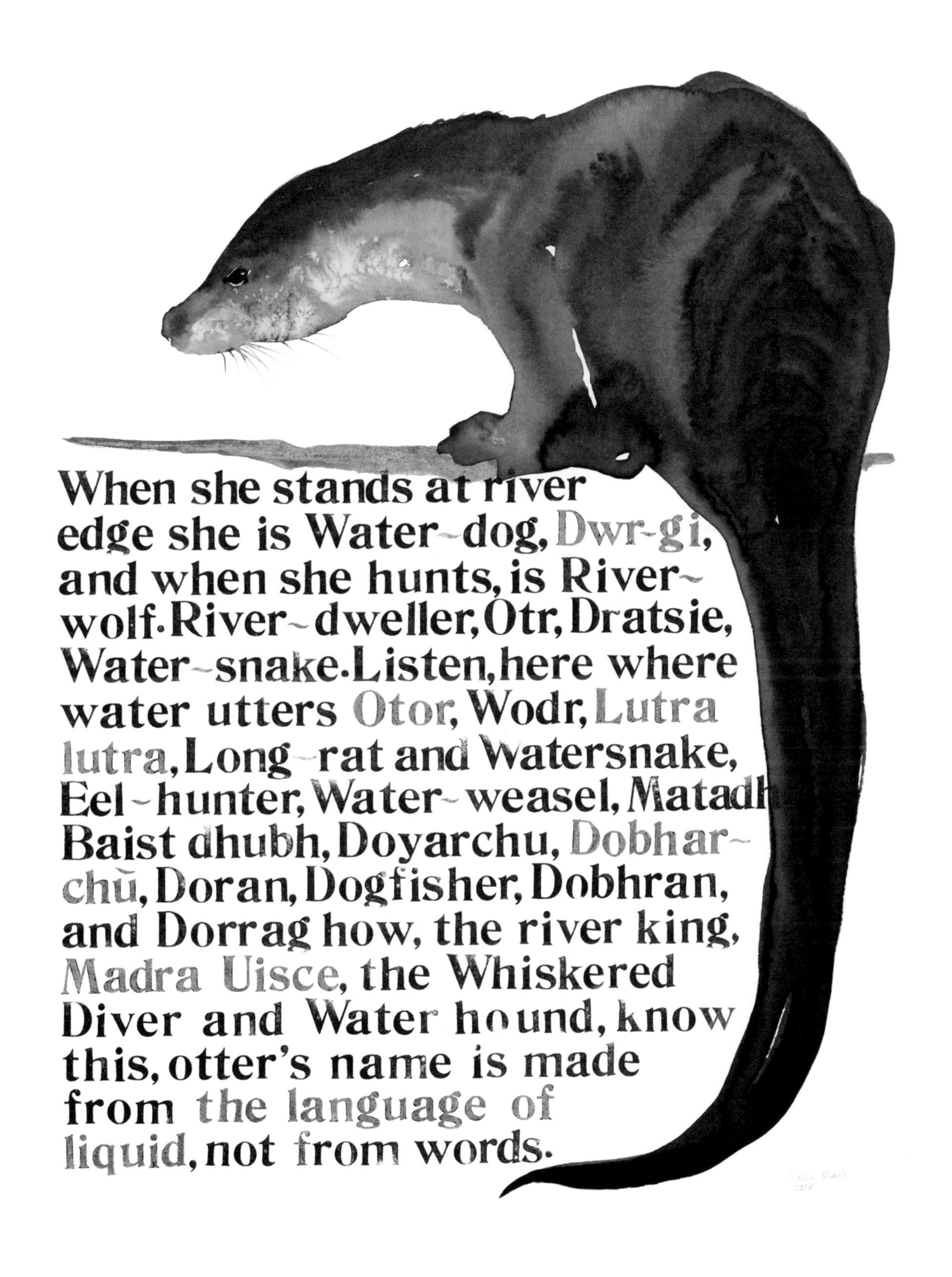
When she stands at river
edge she is Water-dog, Dwr-gi,
and when she hunts, is River-
wolf. River-dweller, Otr, Dratsie,
Water-snake. Listen, here where
water utters Otor, Wodr, Lutra
lutra, Long-rat and Watersnake,
Eel-hunter, Water-weasel, Matadh
Baist dhubh, Doyarchu, Dobhar-
chú, Doran, Dogfisher, Dobhran,
and Dorrag how, the river king,
Madra Uisce, the Whiskered
Diver and Water hound, know
this, otter's name is made
from the language of
liquid, not from words.

Wild.

Even as a child I dreamed of otters, wanting not to own an otter as a pet but to be an otter. To shape-shift into an otter pelt.

Words at one time swam for me like otters through rivers of pages. Learning to read, learning to write, neither was easy. Trying to copy those forms that made no sense, seemed so abstract – unable to understand how they joined to form words, linked to words I heard spoken, words in the ear, words in the eye. Even when the trick of it was caught, the words continued to swim in the mind's eye. Even when I knew they were fixed on the page, they would ripple and twine, and I thought this was how all people saw written words. It made it hard to read aloud when words moved and you had to catch them first. A hunger for stories taught me the trick of it.

And, at the end of the day, handwriting, once you know the shape of the letters and how they fit together, is all just drawing words.

Painting otters, trying to learn their shape and movement, then wishing to write in otters, continues to teach me about reading, writing.

The twenty-six otters of the alphabet seem to be a natural script – a different shape, a wilder code. Learning to read in otter, to write in otter, is no more difficult than this trick that the majority of the UK population take for granted, while the rest cannot fully take part in the glorious alchemical pleasure of reading, excluded from a literate society, excluded from reading this. At times it seems to me this literacy is a tyranny. Those who cannot manage to learn the trick, often through no fault of their own, are marginalised, often humiliated, left to cope alone. Around half of prisoners in the UK are functionally illiterate, and the number continues to rise.

The twenty-six otters of the alphabet are teaching me again about writing, as I print out an alphabet with rubber stamps, as I handwrite calligraphic river gods in river water and sumi ink.

And I understand also that I am still learning to read, not taking for granted how those twenty-six letters move into my mind, building worlds and people, made of ink, easing my soul.

I am glad to have seen wild otters, in rivers, in the sea, in my mind's eye. Even more, am I glad that I learned the trick of the literate. Now I try to join the two in a dancing script, as otter souls swim into words.

Photographs of British Algæ.

Cyanotype Impressions.

The difficulty of making accurate drawings of objects so minute as many
f the Algæ and Confervæ, has induced me to avail myself of Sir John
Herschel's beautiful process of Cyanotype, to obtain impressions of the
lants themselves, which I have much pleasure in offering to my botanical
iends.

I hope that *in general* the impressions will be found sharp and
ell defined, but in some instances (such as the Fuci) the thickness of the
pecimens renders it impossible to press the glass used in taking Photographs
ufficiently close to them to ensure a perfect representation of every part.
eing however unwilling to omit any species to which I had access, I
have preferred giving such impressions as I *could* obtain of these thicker
bjects, to their entire omission. I take this opportunity of returning
ny thanks to the friends who have allowed me to use their collections
f Algæ on this occasion.

The names refer to Harvey's "Manual of British Algæ". I
have taken the Tribes and Species in their proper order when I was
ble to do so, but in many cases I have been compelled to make long
eaps, from the want of the plants that should have been next inserted,
nd in this first number I have intentionally departed from the
ystematic arrangement, that I might give specimens of very various
characters as a sample.

A. A.

IMPRESSIONS OF THE SUN

A WOMAN OF ART AND SCIENCE

Words: Annie Worsley
Cyanotypes: Anna Atkins

Botanist Anna Atkins harnessed nineteenth-century technology to frame the future of nature photography and scientific illustration whilst breaking the mould of who could tell the story of natural history.

On a spring day, in the sweet clear air of the Scottish Highlands when humidity is relatively low, two things happen. Firstly, hue and chroma of distant mountain ranges sift through various shades of blue as their overlapping shapes dilute or deepen depending on the viewer's relative perspective. Secondly, the sky above runs from a thick sweep of cyan into a Prussian blue so deep it seems to reveal the very edges of space. Blue is the colour of great distance and enormous depth, and of atmospheric emptiness and oceanic vastness. It has long-standing cultural associations with royalty and power yet connotations of loneliness and sadness. But blue also has an innate magic of its own, with overtones of purity and clarity. It is my favourite colour.

On one of our recent surprisingly pellucid dry days, a rich blue sky mantle arced over the brightening meadows. A single small cloud-surprise sailed by and I photographed it. The image was like an old-fashioned negative, a white ghostly shape against a dark background. The camera had captured the cloud's rapidly changing detail. For a few moments I was thrust back to my childhood, trying to identify animals in clouds as I lay in the grass a long, long time ago. By the time I had looked up from camera to sky, the cloud had vanished and over my head was a dome painted thickly in lapis lazuli.

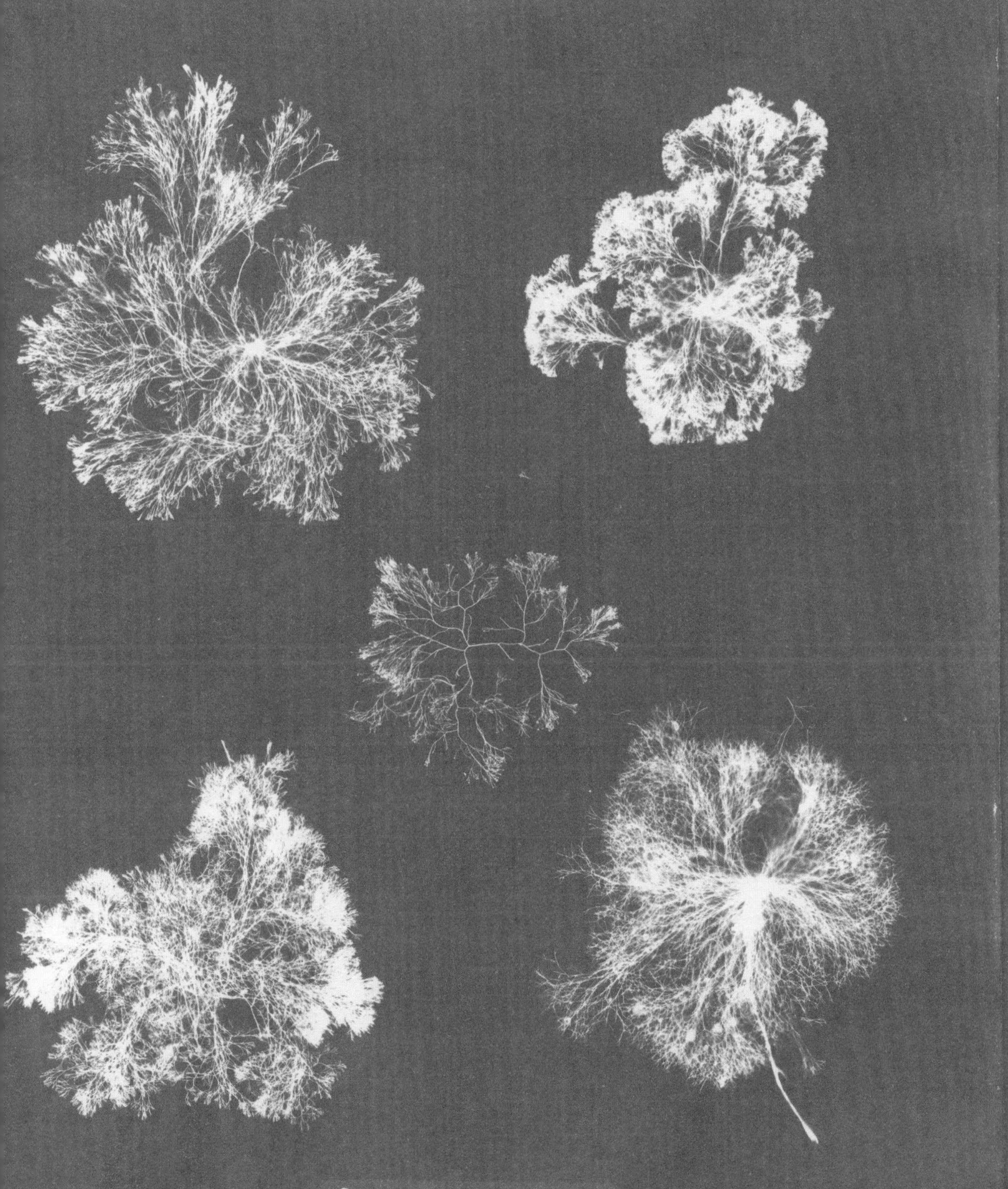

Polysiphonia fastigiata.

Those few minutes spent remembering clouds that were rabbits or flowers and wondering about the blue of vanishing and empty skies reminded me of a woman in science who created beautiful cloud-white images on royal-rich blue paper, the very same colours of my morning sky. Anna Atkins was a remarkable natural historian whose spectacular work both influenced perceptions of imagery and colour and revitalised the traditional methods of scientific observation and classification through her seminal work on algae. I saw copies of her images as an undergraduate student – they were secreted in an old book I had randomly picked from the university library because I liked the cover. Most pictures in the book were hand drawn in black ink, but several unusual blue-and-white plates caught my attention. At the time I had not heard of cyanotypes or Atkins but I was thrilled by the pictures' luscious, vivid yet stark clarity. A few years later as I began my doctoral research, using pollen to determine vegetation composition in New Guinea, I wished that somehow my pollen grains could be presented in the same way: as white graphics against a blue background. Of course it was not to be, although today colleagues can use very sophisticated electronic microscopes to display pollen and other plant tissues in a whole array of dazzling colours.

Anna Atkins was a woman of science in a different era. She was born in 1799, and some 150 years before I was drawing plant structures she had crafted the illustrations for her father's translation of *Genera of Shells* by Lamarck. At a time when photography was in its infancy, capturing the shapes and details of fauna and flora in pencil, ink and paint was critical. Learning to observe and draw the life form before you was fundamental to understanding the shape of organisms in the natural world. Art and science in the nineteenth century were conjoined – each supported and necessitated the other. By the time I was a student, they had diverged and textbooks were filled with photographs, diagrams and data. It was only when I came to undertake a PhD – learning to identify pollen grains – that I took up the pencil and drew what I saw under the microscope. For most in science, the artistic skills of drawing had long since been abandoned in favour of the photographic lens and measuring equipment. ➳

Polysiphonia Brodiæi

Grateloupia filicina.

Sporochnus pedunculatus.

Atkins' father was a respected scientist who believed in encouraging his daughter's interest in botany and natural history, though both her fascination and his advocacy were highly unusual for the time. Through her father's contacts at the Royal Society, Atkins learned about William Henry Fox Talbot's invention of 'photograms' and, just a few years later, of John Herschel's refinement of the Talbot process, which he named the 'cyanotype'. Atkins quickly realised that, even in comparison with her considerable artistic and recording skills, the new method had the potential to capture much more detail, and with much greater speed. The process was simple. It involved the application of two chemical compounds to a sheet of paper, which was then dried. A plant or other object was placed on the paper, and the two were left in full sunlight. After a time the chemicals were washed away with water to leave a clear, white image against a background of blue. By the time Atkins was learning how to undertake the creation of a cyanotype, she had developed a lifelong love of algae. As the two interests came together, her greatest work began.

Over more than a decade, Atkins produced thousands of images, principally of algae, that would come together in her substantial book *Photographs of British Algae*. Some of the most ethereal and wondrous images of coastal algae, the seaweeds, are entrained in deep oceanic blues as breathtakingly detailed white or cream ghosts. There are tendrils, feathers, lace, filaments and dendrites – structures so delicate that some details would normally only be observed using a hand lens, but somehow they are conveyed by the contrast between two simple colours. Not only did Atkins perfect the technique but in each image she also displayed her considerable artistic and scientific prowess – by placing and arranging the algae carefully, she revealed their intricacies and inner mysteries.

Atkins' books on algae are magical. The elemental energy of a single species is recorded in its cloud-shape on every sky-page. It is as if the inner structures and workings of each alga are laid bare for all to see. And most of all, though scientifically intimate, the images are individual works of art crafted by a woman who, years ahead of her time, knew the very essence and shape of the natural world around her. I suspect she too had spent time watching clouds pass by in a piercingly blue spring sky, naming the creatures they created before they vanished. How wonderful that her life's works should include records of shapes most of us would find impossible to imagine, let alone identify.

Cystoseira fibrosa.

WILD AMATEURS

ON WRITING AND WOODWORK

Words: Wyl Menmuir
Photography: Jay Armstrong

When a novelist attempts to craft a desk, he judges the result beautifully flawed but entirely pleasing. Working in wood, making things that occupy space in the world, becomes a counterpoint to the formlessness of fiction.

When I finish writing my first novel, I am out of words – I have emptied what feels like my entire store of them into the strange story that has dominated my life for three years, and I'm in need of something else to nourish me until I'm ready to start the next. I wrote much of my first novel with my notebook balanced on my knees, while I was in my campervan or on the train, or sitting on the sofa after the children had gone to bed. If I am going to write another, I figure, I will definitely need a desk.

I scout around and, aside from one made by a local carpenter and artist that is a good thousand pounds more than I can afford, I see little that fits the idea of the desk I have in my head. I want something solid and simple, and as I think I sketch three planks strapped together on two trestles. I imagine what it will look like finished, with an Anglepoise lamp in one corner, a cup of coffee and a ream of paper on which I have written the first draft of my second novel – and I decide to make it myself. After all, how hard can it be?

I track down a cabinetmaker who is getting rid of the contents of his workshop and he sells me two planks of English elm that are gathering dust. He asks what I want the wood for and I explain my plan, adding that I think it will take me about half a day to saw it into shape and sand it down, and that by evening it should be finished. He looks doubtful and asks how I plan to cut the wood to length. How will I brace the planks? How do I plan on preventing the wood from bowing? When I explain that I am going to use a handsaw and that I am sure I'll work the rest out, he sighs and puts the kettle on, and we spend the rest of the afternoon cutting the wood to size in the workshop. He patiently shows me how to match the grain and draws an arcane shape onto the underside of the planks. At first I assume this is something superstitious, but he explains that it makes the loose planks into a jigsaw that I can reassemble later, a cabinetmaker's clever trick. He is sure, he says, that I know I need to use a wood stronger than that of the main desk to brace it, and before I leave he slips two short lengths of oak and a pair of saw horses into my van, clearly despairing of my plan to do the rest of the work on the kitchen table.

With the first obstacles dealt with, I think it will then be a simple case of screwing the whole thing together, a bit of sanding and a lot of standing back to admire my handiwork. It actually takes me about five weeks. I realise quickly that I still have no idea how I am going to smooth the planks into a flat surface on which to write. And then there are the thousand things I don't know that I need to know: how to screw into the wood without splitting it (it involves candle wax); how to actually brace the planks (I had nodded as if I'd understood entirely as the cabinetmaker had explained it to me – he'd probably have put his head in his hands if he'd known that I would strap the planks together with gaffer tape to hold them in place while I worked on them); and how to finish the edges with chamfering (which is a word I don't even know yet). Then there's the coming to terms with the fact of the timber. Come across a knot and you'll have to find a way of incorporating it into the design. Cut against the grain and you'll hack out lumps of wood.

As I make progress on the desk, I discover the elm has had, at some point, an infestation of woodworm, and one end of the plank is so riddled that part of it collapses in on itself. I persevere, sanding out the resulting bowl in the wood and naming it 'the ashtray', determined that it will be a feature. Sanding is a meditation. I stand over the planks for hours going down through grades of sandpaper before I realise how little progress I am making and discover the joys of the orbital sander. At some point, the grain starts to blur in the most wonderful way.

I've since discovered that most carpenters try to avoid this happening, but I encourage it. I let it take its own shape and marvel at the patterns that emerge. Later, I bring out the grain with beeswax, which fills in some of the holes I've opened up, and polish for hours. I seek help from both my father-in-law and another friendly carpenter. I watch countless how-to videos and consult a retired boat builder, who looks at my work in progress, manages not to laugh at my ineptitude and gives me a whole list of next steps and advice. My various mentors assist me patiently as I set out on what I now think of as an ongoing, and incredibly slow-burning, apprenticeship.

I have no particular hope that I will ever get beyond this apprenticeship. I am doing it mostly for the joy of it and, anyway, the stakes of this project are so much lower than those of my novel. My desk and all the woodwork projects I've undertaken since have been purely for my own amusement. They do not exist to please anyone else and I don't intend to sell the things I make, nor would I expect anyone to want to buy them. To me, though, they are beautifully flawed and entirely pleasing in and of themselves. And I figured that if I screwed up the desk I could buy a sheet of plywood and it would fulfil the same purpose. The lightness with which I approached the project meant the pressure was off, and it made working on the desk more pleasure than chore.

My desk takes shape in a way that a novel doesn't. After every session, I'm able to see the changes I'm imposing. Every cut I make, every hour of sanding, brings a new dimension to my handiwork. Writing a novel is a process of thousands of tiny incremental amendments, and over the course of a few hours of writing or editing I might not see much change. Some days a good session involves me having moved forty words around the page, and even then it's often unclear to me whether I've made it better or worse. The pleasure of working with wood is to see it take shape before your eyes as you work it, whether that shape is a fish emerging from a small lump of wood or a plank becoming a desk.

Poet Holly Corfield Carr, a self-confessed 'wild amateur' woodworker, once reimagined a life in which she would spend half her time devoted to poetry and the rest to carpentry. 'The limit and the shape of what I make are determined by the material in the same way that my poems are determined – in terms of their size, shape and form – by those spaces in which I find them,' she tells me when we meet to discuss a shared love of woodwork and words.

The objects that Holly makes are entirely determined by the wood she finds in her home city of Bristol, where the streets are generous with abandoned furniture. ⤚

SOFT
"SC"
D

'I'm currently making a chest of drawers out of a bed frame, to practise my dovetailing,' she says. 'I found the bed on the street and I don't need another bed, but I do need a chest of drawers. I've not quite made the chest yet, but I've made the "of drawers". The limit and the shape of what I make are determined by the material in the same way that my poems are determined – in terms of their size, shape and form – by those spaces in which I find them. The other thing I really enjoy is collecting tools. My poetry tools are things I can't necessarily see. I can't put them in a small display, which is perhaps why the paraphernalia of carpentry interests me.'

Holly later shows me a selection of bevel edge chisels, which she refers to by the names of the carpenters who previously owned them, names that are stamped on their handles: Pritchard, Shifnal and Rolfe.

'I enjoy handling these tools and thinking, "What am I going to make with these?"' she says. 'The answer is there in the wood. It's the literalism of them that interests me.'

Perhaps it is this literalism that draws writers towards more physical crafts, from the heft of the tools to the undeniable solidity of the evidence of work – the desk or the chair, the garden or the painted canvas. Working with one's hands can serve as a balance to dealing with concepts and elusive ideas, the physical as counterbalance to the uncertain mental stumble through the metaphorical woods that so often represents the writing process.

There is something in Holly's acceptance of the materials as the starting point that strikes home. The materials themselves afford or constrain different forms of expression, while suggesting and influencing form. The material resistance you encounter when you work with wood or plants, wool or lino, is more definite and at the same time somehow easier to contend with than the resistance of words. When you make a cut, there's no going back.

When I start on a new piece of fiction, everything is formless and in the writing process I inevitably become lost before I am able to find an outline for the story I want to tell. It can be slow and often tortuous. I wait for things to come into focus, suggestions of shape. With wood, I understand at the outset what I'm aiming for – whether it comes out that way is another matter, but I can see the progress with each pass of the blade over the wood. I balance an uncertain practice with making real things that occupy space in the world – a desk, a knife handle (there's a wonderful circularity in crafting a knife for whittling with a whittling knife), a spoon, a coffee table, a leather knife sheath and several small wooden chess pieces that resemble hybrid animals of the sort that are mainly found in the margins of medieval manuscripts. I finish them in a matter of hours or weeks, as opposed to the years I might spend on a novel. I care for these things in a way I could never care for anything I bought in a shop, and in an entirely different way too. And, by way of contradiction, I'm also less precious about them. The mug rings and the palimpsest effect of writing on a waxed surface add to the story of the desk and I do nothing to stop the proliferation of either. My desk will always be wonky and my knife set at an angle that would make a professional cutler wince, but I have found that there is something of real value to be gained by engaging with the underlying philosophy of bringing something physical into being. Perhaps something is learned from one that is indirectly transferred to the other. Perhaps underlying both is a more general philosophy of creating, what might be termed a unity of internal procedure.

As I write these words, I run my hands over the undulations and imperfections of the desk I made and balance a biro, nib down, in one of the many exit holes the woodworms have left. It should be deflating to have put so much time into something and to have ended up with a desk that falls short of performing the one function for which it is designed – to be a flat surface on which to write. However, the building of the desk was the start of a practice that has become an antidote to a day spent with words, a way to use a different part of my mind, a very different sort of creativity.

I find working with wood reassuring in a way that working with words cannot be. However hard I try to make words mean what I want them to mean, they are at best a representation. That's the challenge of words. The challenge of working with materials is something else – it is to discover the haecceity, the 'thisness', the qualities and characteristics that make this physical thing exactly the thing it is. But it is also the connection to the solid world of planes; to chisels on which are stamped the owner's name; to saws, benches, routers and laser cutters; to wood, lino, leather and fabric. And, to be simplistic about it, it's fun. Like any activity that takes you out of yourself, any activity that absorbs your concentration fully and with space for no other concerns, it feeds your creative work. There is a sense in which these physical activities provide balance for the mental work of writing – a sense in which they can, in a number of ways, nourish the creative process. You know that when you return to your desk (however uneven and woodwormy) the words will be there again, waiting to be written.

Wood moves with time. It shrinks and swells. What looks flat and straight to begin with warps and settles over weeks and months. Where small cracks open out, I learn how to make a paste of glue and wood dust to fill them, and when I move the desk into the house it looks perfectly level. For all of two days. Then it starts to move more dramatically, twisting even the oak braces. Now I can post pound coins into the gaps between the planks. There's an acceptance of this change, the realisation that you are only partly in control of the process and that you have to give yourself over to this mutability, accept that some processes are beyond your control. This feels somehow liberating, and I am, perhaps, more forgiving of my other mistakes as a result. Perhaps, I start to think, I should also try being more forgiving of my words.

PINNACLE OF PERFECTION

THE POINT OF A GUILLEMOT EGG

Words: Tim Birkhead
Illustration: Georgie Bennett

There are few more remarkable birds than the guillemot, and little to rival the artistry of its eggs, each one unique in colour and with infinite variations of squiggle and swirl. Several explanations have been put forward for why natural selection has created such an exquisite design.

L

The beauty of birds' eggs has inspired me as a scientist. Beauty lies in the eye of the beholder, and my notion of what is beautiful includes not only the physical appearance of eggs but also the way natural selection has created such apparent perfection.

A bird's egg is the most remarkable combination of adaptations. These adaptations allow them to be laid and incubated in an incredible diversity of habitats and nest types – from the snug, feather-lined cups of long-tailed tit nests to the filthy rock ledges of seabird colonies. It is little wonder that Thomas Wentworth Higginson, a nineteenth-century abolitionist better known for his campaigning for the rights of women and other disenfranchised people than for his deep love of nature, said that 'if required on pain of death to name instantly the most perfect thing in the universe, I should risk my fate on a birds' egg'. I agree, which is why I titled my book on the biology of eggs *The Most Perfect Thing*.

Writing about birds' eggs was dangerous, I knew. Many have been misled by conservation organisations into thinking that eggs are a no-go area. Egg collecting, once widespread, was made illegal in the UK, quite rightly, in 1954, as part of a broader and essential process of protecting bird populations. Such is the feeling still that one conservation organisation, fearful that the book might incite a resurgence of collecting, banned *The Most Perfect Thing* from their bookshops – at least until some of their own members pointed out that this was rather silly.

Collecting was a Victorian vice. During the era of egg collecting, which ran from the 1820s through to 1954, numerous bird books were published, many of them illustrated with exquisite oological images. Very often the frontispiece or *pièce de résistance* of these books was an illustration of a guillemot's egg – a clear indication that the ovarian output of this particular species was the egg collector's pinnacle of perfection.

For me too, a guillemot's egg represents an example of biological perfection. I started to study guillemots on Skomer, an island off the coast of Pembrokeshire, in 1972, and I have been back each year since, to understand how guillemot populations work and to protect them. My first view of a guillemot's egg left me amazed by its size, shape and colour. They are huge – the human equivalent of a sixteen-pound baby – but they are also the most extraordinary shape, sharply pointed at one end. Their colour, though, is what particularly distinguishes them – every egg is unique, each one a veritable Jackson Pollock of dark blotches, squiggles and swirls superimposed on a ground of white, sky blue and turquoise through to dark green.

The brilliance of an egg at the moment it emerges from a female guillemot's body is startling. This was how I felt when I first experienced this sight – the newly laid egg so vibrantly turquoise I wondered how on earth such colours could be created. As it lay on one of the monochrome, mucky ledges on which guillemots breed, it positively glowed.

As well as celebrating those three features of guillemot eggs – their size, colour and shape – biologists ask 'why' and 'how'. This inquisitiveness is probably inherent. I knew from a very early age that a sensory appreciation of the natural world was, on its own, not enough. But I also knew that a hard-nosed scientific approach wasn't either. I wanted to embrace both cultures, with each enriching and reinforcing the other in an endless interplay of aesthetics and information.

Guillemot eggs are relatively large because the chick has to hatch at an advanced stage of development, and that is best done by providing it with a lot of food, in the form of a large yolk. This, in combination with an adequate supply of albumen, determines the size of the egg.

What the earlier oologists found so seductive about guillemot eggs was their colour variation. Each female lays an egg whose colour and pattern are unique to her. But why? The answer is that this allows each female to know her own egg and to ensure that she and her partner rear their own offspring and not one of their neighbour's. Remarkably, the seemingly infinite variation in the colour of birds' eggs is created from a very limited palette – just two pigments, one reddish, one greenish, mixed in different proportions and layered on at different densities to generate an entire spectrum. How the marks are applied is a mystery for some future egg enthusiast to solve.

The shape of birds' eggs is exquisite. Allow a 'mere' supermarket chicken egg to lie in your hand. Close your eyes and curl your fingers around the egg, feeling its elliptical curves. Perfection. Now imagine that sensation magnified three times, as though you have a guillemot's egg in your palm. It seems heavy, and that pointed shape moulds to your hand in the most remarkably tactile way. Again, the 'how' remains a mystery: we are still trying to understand the internal processes that produce this extraordinary shape.

The 'why' of the shape has spawned a number of ideas, revealing in the process the gullibility of the human mind and our predisposition to believe what we wish to be true. The first idea to be put forward was that the pointed shape allowed a guillemot egg to spin like a top (albeit on its side) when knocked or blown by the wind. This turned out to be naive – for indeed a museum egg will spin, but only because it is an empty, virtually weightless shell. The second idea, 'rolling in an arc', is the most pervasive and persistent of guillemot-egg-shape beliefs – but again it has no evidence. Place an intact guillemot's egg on a slightly tilted tabletop and release it, and it will roll in an arc. Do the same with the egg of a razorbill (the guillemot's closest cousin, which doesn't breed on narrow cliff ledges and whose egg is not pointed and more closely resembles a chickens egg in shape) and it will roll in a straight line. The reasoning seemed clear – the assumption was made that, by rolling in an arc, the guillemot's egg is saved from falling directly off the ledge.

But no. The experiment must be done properly, by repeating the test with the eggs of both species on dozens of different *natural* ledges. The shape of the egg makes no difference. A guillemot's pointed egg will rarely roll in an arc, and it won't be saved. Moreover, many guillemot ledges are much narrower than the area of the arc created by the egg on a smooth surface. Not only that, but guillemots invariably position their eggs on the ledge so that the pointed end is towards the sea, so that if knocked it rolls *outwards* towards the cliff edge – exactly the opposite of what one might expect if the pointed shape had evolved to prevent the eggs from rolling into oblivion.

With my colleagues, I have spent the past five years thinking of other explanations for the pointedness of guillemot eggs, and after much effort we think we have the answer. Our research shows that a pointed egg is simply more stable – especially on the sloping ledges that guillemots often breed upon – and a stable egg is more safely manipulated by parent birds. The pointed shape does help the guillemot egg to remain on the ledge, but not by spinning or rolling – simply because it makes it less likely to roll in the first place.

My focus on guillemot eggs is part of a broader vision. Like many seabirds, guillemots are in trouble, from climate change, oil pollution and over-fishing. Most guillemot populations in the UK are in decline, although so far, at least, those on Skomer are thriving. We know this only because researchers like myself have devised ways of accurately monitoring their numbers, how long they live, how many offspring they produce and what kinds of fish they feed their chicks. I have monitored Skomer's guillemots since the 1980s on a modest budget, which in its wisdom the Welsh government decided to terminate in 2014.

Reluctant to accept that my work would be compromised by lack of funds, I started a crowdfunding campaign and in 2015 raised enough to keep the study going for a further five years. The messages of goodwill from donors were utterly inspirational and I will continue to fight for guillemots into the future. There are few more remarkable birds than the guillemot, and few more remarkable sensations than being in one of their huge, thriving colonies. Less colourful and comical than the puffin, which everyone loves, guillemots excel on so many other levels, from their sophisticated social lives and charitable care of each other's offspring to the sheer artistry of their pyriform eggs.

Lying amidst the muck and squalor of a typical breeding ledge, the guillemot's vibrantly coloured egg rests beneath its parent as a symbol of hope for the future.

WILD SERVICE

A POEM BY WILL BURNS

Illustration: Neil Gower

The late July days. Dragonfly days like
fat, when even the river played itself
in halftime, air so thick it had killed birdsong.

I lost the river path, lay on my back
under a wild service tree, my shirt cool
from sweat. I could feel there would be thunder
on its given day, that would seem to mean
no more than domestic grief and headaches –
broken bricks and roof tiles, shattered timber.

We were hundreds of miles apart
and despite my holding onto some dull hope,
as stilled and desperate as the stream itself,
I suppose you decided in the end
that it was just too far for you to come.

Wild Service
NG

A MODERN BOOK OF HOURS

AN ARTIST CONTEMPLATES THE CADENCES OF DAY AND NIGHT

Words & Illustration: Rebecca Clark
Illuminations: Anonymous, Fifteenth Century

It was the winter of 2007 when I first saw curator John Hand's extraordinary exhibition *Prayers and Portraits: Unfolding the Netherlandish Diptych* at the National Gallery of Art in Washington, DC. Installed in one intimate space were works by some of the great northern European painters of the fifteenth and sixteenth centuries – Robert Campin, Jan van Eyck, Rogier van der Weyden, Hugo van der Goes, Albrecht Bouts, Quentin Massys. On display were luminous and exquisitely rendered panel paintings – medieval Christian diptychs intended to be used for meditation and contemplation. The labour that had gone into each realistic detail was cause enough for awe, but their clear, rich pigments – applied with such subtlety – felt transcendental.

Housed in beautifully crafted wooden frames assembled with hinges and clasps, each one contained a mysterious enclosed world. Handheld diptychs from this period were designed to be experienced like a book: opened, viewed, then closed and clasped shut, demanding a personal and direct experience. Unlike the more dramatic and emotionally charged religious paintings from southern Europe, the art of the northern Renaissance was relatively reserved and reflective. The human subjects seem to carry a quiet acceptance of grief and a resignation to sorrow. It is as if they possess some deep understanding of It All. This sensibility resonated with me because my own work straddles a line between realism and the metaphysical, within a context of loss.

Seeing these works for the very first time, what struck me most was the dichotomy between the small scale of the diptychs and the quiet power that emanated from them. In today's age of bold, supersized, extravagant art, this exhibition was a welcome understatement. I walked away carrying a blessing, a secret, an inner glow.

In the following weeks, especially as I rode the DC Metro to and from work on my daily commute, I became acutely aware of how deeply absorbed people become when hooked up to their handheld digital devices, heads bowed above the glow, completely entranced. There is an intense devotional quality about it. The vehicles through which people in the fifteenth and twenty-first centuries receive their rapture are similar – both viewing experiences are framed within a box and, with an iPad in a case, a box that opens and closes, much like a diptych. Both emit a glow; both demand singular attention. These observations stayed with me and I began to think about how I could create a contemporary version of an illuminated devotional to be viewed on a digital tablet.

➳

Domine ne in fu
rore tuo arguas
me neqꝫ in ira
tua corripias me

Matins

None

Vespers

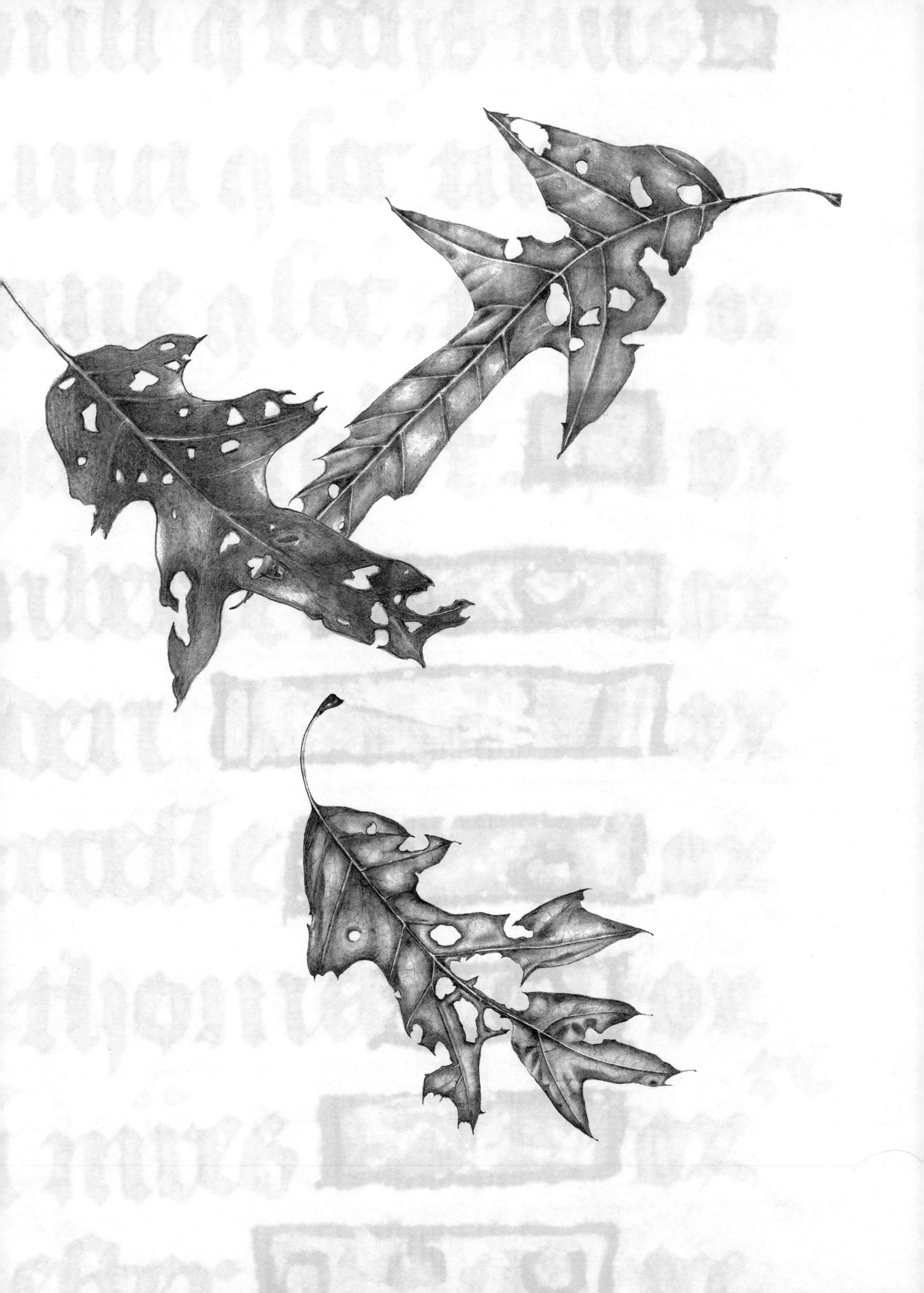

Vigils

non comminuetis ex eo Et iterũ
alia scriptura dixit Videbunt in
quẽ trãsfixerunt. Post hec autem
rogauit pylatũ ioseph ab arima-
thia: eo ꝙ esset discipulus ihũ
occultus autem propter metũ
iudeorum vt tolleret corpus
ihũ z permisit pylatus. Venit
ergo: z tulit corpus ihũ. Venit
autem z nichodemus qui venerat
ad ihm nocte primũ ferens mix
turam mirre et aloes quasi li
bras centum. Acceperũt ergo cor
pus ihũ z ligauerunt eum lin
theis cum aromatibz: sicut mos
iudeis est sepelire. Erat autem
locus vbi crucifixus est ortus. z
in orto monumentũ nouũ: in
quo nundum quisq̃ positus fue
rat. Ibi ergo propter parasceuẽ
iudeorum: quia iuxta erant
monumentum: posuerunt ihm.
Deo gratias ꝑ euangelica dicta de
leantur nr̃a peccata. Amen.

Like diptychs, medieval books of hours are devotionals, intimate in scale and portable, but they include text, prayers and psalms in addition to images. As so much of my inspiration for my own art derives from poetry, prose and music, I concluded that modelling my project after books of hours was a perfect solution. Intrigued by the practice of the Benedictine monks, who pray at different hours for different purposes, in the months following my visit to the *Prayers and Portraits* exhibition I began to see that my studio practice had developed a devotional quality that echoed the mood of the time of day and the season. Each season and time has an equal value, and, as I spent time drawing in these hours over the seasons, I began to appreciate the beauty of the different times of day.

In the early morning and in spring, when life is wakening, there is a freshness and a calm – new birth, youth and hope of returning warmth. These became my Matins drawings. In the afternoon, the summertime of the day, there's work to be done and the mood of the day is more rational. There is full light, a sense of maturing, bold and bright colours. These drawings became None (or Nones). In the evening and in the fall, Vespers, there's a fading, an ageing. Shadows lengthen, there is a sense of impending sadness, colours start to pale. It is a softer, quieter, and more reflective and contemplative time. My drawings for Vigils, the night-time devotions, are more stark, bleak and heavy like midwinter. There is a cold and a darkness, an acknowledgement of death.

As I worked over the months, the drawings for my own book of hours started to group into these four chapters, seasons and times. I saw a rhythm of light and dark emerge, from the shape of a day, of a year, of a lifetime. I began to appreciate more the quiet message carried by the medieval books of hours, fascinated that in them were 'rules' – psalms and prayers to be sung or chanted aloud at a particular time of day or night – and that there was text and then also illumination. In many ways they are interdisciplinary – a medieval multimedia platform. Mixing music and art and words together has always appealed to me and music is my greatest source of inspiration.

Drawing whilst listening to music helps to silence the internal chatter in my own head and ushers me into an entirely different realm. Over the years, I've collected the songs I've found most conducive to drawing and organised them into playlists according to times of the day: 'Morning', 'Afternoon', 'Evening' and 'Night'. These playlists became the structure of my studio practice and the foundation for this book of hours. In time, merely hearing that sweeping upswing of Ravi Shankar's shimmering sitar opening in 'Friar Park' began to trigger a response in me to put pencil to paper. I came to think of certain bands and musicians as occupying specific phases of the day, and I am now most inspired to draw at dawn and dusk – 'that lovely liminal time', writes Jeanette Winterson on winter, 'where light and dark are hinged against each other'. Perhaps this is an appropriate metaphor for my book of hours, a hinging together of light and dark and every value in between.

It has taken me two years to complete this book of hours and now anyone with an internet connection can view it for themselves. It is a standalone work of collaborative writing and art, and it is also autobiographical, as each element reflects the daily reality of my own creative process, both in thought and in practice. I also wonder whether it is a guide for the days ahead: an hourly reminder of the often overlooked beauty of time and season; an acknowledgement of the interconnectedness of all living things and a plea to value the lives of the animals with whom, as temporary visitors on planet Earth, we share time and space; a *memento mori* for this age of the Anthropocene and, hopefully, a vehicle for transcendence.

Often when we speak of the Anthropocene – the age of humans – we speak in terms of damage and plastic waste, but humans also create art, order and good governance, respond to beauty, and express themselves with song. For me, the structure of the book of hours encompasses all of this humanness. Encountering the work of the medieval artists and poets has been an awakening, and this offering – my modern book of hours – is a hymn to human creativity.

MAPPING A POEM

A GUIDE THROUGH UNCERTAIN TERRITORY

Words: Jane Lovell
Artist: Tor Falcon

Fate seeks us out, and then we have only the anchor of words and landscapes, real and metaphorical. There is security in their familiar shape, symmetry and regularity of pattern and form. And, on the path from the dark hours to a sunlit sky, a poem emerges.

In a small room, a tired man shows us slides: curls of bone and something spiralling like DNA. He has no answers. Each time we see him there are fewer possibilities; there are words we must assimilate. I have become a collector of such words: 'spiculated', 'metastatic', 'extensive'. Words we will not use or discuss beyond this room. And then one day we are given 'equivocal'. It bobbles on a nasty wire alongside 'malignant'. We hold our breath. It's new and bears a glimmer of hope. Suddenly we find ourselves in a place from which different paths might emerge. There is no element of choice but there are possibilities, albeit small ones. In these situations, 'vanishingly small' still gives a tangible, if feeble, ember to hold between our fingers, to breathe on, very gently, so that it remains lit.

I look it up to be sure. 'Equivocal': open to more than one interpretation; ambiguous.

In the darkness of the early hours, I write the beginning of a poem.

> *Light spills both ways:*
> *silhouetting stands of blackthorn on the lane*
>
> > *and climbing the slow hill, striping the turf, its grey horse*
> > *racing a big sky*

To fix our strange new landscape, I need concrete images: a slow hill, a grey horse, a big sky. Simple language. A picture of a safe place, if only temporarily so. The need to secure this, to locate it in a rural setting, echoes a long tradition of writing that associates the countryside with safety and tranquillity. Henry Williamson sought healing in the depths of North Devon after returning from the horror of the Western Front; William Wordsworth, made almost physically ill by living in the city, escaped to his native Lake District. Although, today, our landscapes are dirtier, our horizons darker, the countryside remains a place of refuge. In his poem 'The Peace of Wild Things', Wendell Berry speaks of waking up with despair and fear of the future. His answer is to 'go and lie down where the wood drake / rests in his beauty on the water'.

Brought up in the centre of a busy Northamptonshire town, my own love of nature arose partly from writers such as Henry Williamson, Alison Uttley and Walter de la Mare – not only their wonder at its quiet beauty but also their relationship with it, its folklore and stories, its rural life and traditions. Its possibilities of solitude. I have childhood memories of walking the fields around Helpston, their ruts of claggy mud and heaps of sugar beet rigid with frost, following long paths that ran along the edge of the Fens with their immense skies and flat open spaces. As we walked, stories were told of a famous poet buried in the churchyard there, a genius who escaped from an asylum to walk eighty miles home. That poet was John Clare, now regarded as one of the most important nineteenth-century English poets, known primarily for his love of the countryside. This was his land; these were his paths and tracks. I was hooked. I read everything I could find. Poetry and landscape merged, became fixed, inseparable.

Clare's childhood countryside was, in fact, far from what had become by the 1970s a bleak, agricultural wasteland; it was vibrant, busy with people working the land, engaged with its elements and its seasons. The gently undulating terrain of limestone grasslands and ancient woodlands was alive with birds and tiny creatures. Clare knew every wildflower, moth and butterfly, and the location of hidden nests; he understood the instinctual behaviour of birds, the features of plant growth and decay. His depth of knowledge and the detail of that knowledge through the changing seasons and their weather patterns was extraordinary. Nothing went unnoticed. His poetry of that time is vibrant with life and detail. In 'The Nightingale's Nest', we see him creeping through 'fern-strewn thorn clumps' to listen to her song, to find her nest, to watch her feed her young. She is elusive. He comments on her separateness:

How curious is the nest; no other bird
Uses such loose materials, or weaves
Its dwelling in such spots: dead oaken leaves
Are placed without, and velvet moss within,
And little scraps of grass, and, scant and spare,
What scarcely seem materials, down and hair;
For from men's haunts she nothing seems to win.

Sadly, it seems that however quietly and separately we live, fate will seek us out. Clare's countryside, and possibly his sanity, was lost to the environmental destruction caused by the Enclosure Acts of the early 1800s. Similarly, we find our own world lost to an alien landscape of consulting rooms and corridors. The nightmare deepens with each investigation and the dread of its results. I write a series of poems that track our lonely journey. They are raw and questioning. Images and themes recur: fireflies represent the nacreous blobs of light on a PET scan; the thrush I hear every morning just before dawn symbolises hope. As time goes on, the poems become increasingly figurative. Some bury themselves so completely in metaphor that they appear on first reading to be solely about the natural world. Some arise from a single word that changes identity through its use in an unfamiliar context: words such as 'ghost', 'fluorescence' and 'equivocal'.

I am not just a collector of words. I surround myself with found objects. They anchor me to something beyond my own shifting and finite existence. The room where I write has glass-topped cases, collectors' cabinets, engravings; on a shelf, a tiny nest of moss and feathers that once belonged to a goldcrest; in a box on the desk, a crow skull, the salt-worn shell of a heart urchin, skeletons of *Physalis franchetti*, each with its own perfect symmetry. There is security in shape, in symmetry, in the regularity of pattern and form. Even the walls harbour curiosities: brilliant cobalt scarabs woven into a net of vole-coloured lace, Japanese clam shells painted with miniature scenes of cherry trees and geishas, a flock of eighteenth-century hummingbirds. Each has a story, a history – a meaning that goes beyond its appearance in the same way that the cover of a familiar book conjures images that could almost be from our own memories. That many of these objects have survived centuries and travelled many miles is not only fascinating but also somehow reassuring.

Mapping a poem, losing oneself in the pathways of its words and syllables, in the tracks of its rhythm, can offer similar sanctuary. Embedding it in nature gives us camouflage. We can hide in its forests, in the shadows of its mountains. In order to convey inevitability and chance, without tempting fate, I bury my poem in a landscape that is seemingly benign: a quiet lane, a hill, a fence. But I need to weave in a dark story, to trace a line between vulnerability and tenacity. This speaks to me of owl.

Researching the origins of an engraving I find in a junk shop, I come across an old French work by Jules Michelet – *L'oiseau*. It tells a story that balances the possibility of survival against the odds, that of a barn owl flying on silent wing while a weasel creeps into the nest:

> *Le chat-huant vole d'une aile silencieuse,*
> *comme étoupée de ouate. La longue*
> *belette s'insinue au nid, sans frôler une feuille.*

For the purposes of my poem, the image is perfect.

I fly my owl along the line of the fence, the early light tracing the edge of her wings. As a counterpoint to her symmetry and calm, I add Michelet's predatory weasel creeping towards the nest. I maintain a detached tone. We are observers, powerless to intervene; the outcome remains uncertain.

> *The weasel creeps to her nest without brushing*
> *a leaf*
> *breathing its pinbone mess of pellet and fur.*

I choose my words carefully. Barn owls' nests are composed of regurgitated pellets, sometimes several years' worth: layers of mess studded with tiny bones and unhatched eggs. An essential element of nature poetry, for me, is that it is grounded in science and natural history, that it is anchored, to some degree, in fact. In the same way that I collect natural objects, I gather information, essays and images from all over the world: myriad minutiae, details that may later be woven into the texture of a poem. They might be about the nesting habits of barn owls or about the shrimp that live their entire lives within the ornate structure of a glass sponge at the bottom of the ocean. Sometimes a story or an image can suddenly spark an entire poem: the horses – put to shelter in a church at Bywell during the great floods of 1771 – that clamped onto the pews with their teeth to save themselves from drowning in the swirling waters; such treasures as Tim Dee's tweeted images of the Madagascan collared nightjar at Tring – 'those are mothballs that were his eyes'; and the arresting headline 'In good years, snowy owls build nests out of dead lemmings' from Sarah Dougherty's article on the Public Radio International website.

Time has passed. The weasel has crept nearer. I want to delay my owl's return to her nest; I want time to contemplate the possibilities of survival before knowing what the future might hold. I switch from weasel to owl and back. The progress of each is purposefully slow. I glance back and forth in the same way that we watch the damsel bound to the railway track and the ever-approaching train that never seems to move significantly closer. Pinbone, pellet, pinpoint, patter... the seconds tick by. The rhythm is kept even. Weasel patter, wingbeat, heartbeat: the inexorable passing of time. Detail about the owl's flight serves to further suspend the outcome.

> *Her ears pinpoint sound in delay; last night's start*
> *and patter, her hunger, buried in the fall of rain.*

The asymmetry of an owl's ears allows for sound localisation. Unfortunately, the tiniest sounds can be lost in the confusion of rainfall and our owl is returning to the nest hungry. In reality, a barn owl will not leave her eggs or her young: she is fed by the male. But there is a darker tale to reveal that is, for the moment, hidden from sight.

Sometimes we need dark tales. Just as children need wolves and witches. Ted Hughes tells some of the darkest and most brutal. In 'February 17th', his tale is of an unborn lamb that becomes jammed in the birth canal. Even in the first lines, there is a tone of finality. By the end of the poem, we are left with the idea of a long miserable trek, a sense of being defeated. But the language is perfect. Like Clare, Hughes worked the land; his landscapes are hard bitten and real. The images may not always be beautiful or the sounds melodic – nature is messy and unkempt, and it follows its own laws – but the detail is brilliant. Hughes and Clare celebrate the essence of wildness. Although from very different worlds, both exhibit a passion and precision, a creativity with language that marks them out. Their influence, certainly on my poetry, is deep rooted. It arises from the mud of ploughed fields and the wind-harried hilltops, from watery marshes below the broad sweep of fenland skies.

Our own dark tale continues, becomes darker. We visit a hospital as big as a planet. Down a long corridor, in a room of moments we shall never forget, a collection of specialists and support staff consider our options, our lack of options. Wheeling up and down the nightscape of an MRI scan, they navigate looming contours of bone, canyons pooling light then shadow. A line of vertebrae flares like comets. Scapula, pelvis, patella bloom and glow. We ask questions. Eyes slide to corners of the room, the space behind us, refusing to gauge the days left to us. We are told 'vanishingly rare'. It may have been quietly invading for years, undetected – but, without a positive diagnosis, no one here can help us.

I finish my poem on the train as I travel to work one cold spring morning. I consider its rhythm, each syllable and its sound, its connections. The owl disappears from sight, leaving silence and a glimmer of wire. I have threaded her own dark story into the landscape. Her own tragedy.

> *In the hedge, something woven from air and*
> *tats of down*
> *is staring, its flyblown carcass stirring as if waking.*

Life is built on bolts of chance. As the owl continues her solitary flight towards an unknown destiny, similarly, our own dark story is not over.

June. A sunlit square in London. The grind and growl of construction, insistent chitchat of sparrows. Stone steps lead into a building that echoes like a library. In a quiet room, a room of angels, we meet a man who speaks of hope. A man who has the answers. He explains that doubling-time can be aggressively fast; it can also be incredibly slow. With the right treatment, it may even be halted.

He offers a new landscape with an altered step of time, a world imaged through the curved eye of a lens. This landscape of light and bone will not change overnight. It has tree lines and hillsides that may well still look the same in many years' time.

Against all odds, the story continues: an owl returning to her nest before the egg is pierced; a time-lapse sky above a slow hill; a landscape fixed by sunlight.

We have our answers. Earth resumes its humming.

Equivocal

Light spills both ways:
silhouetting stands of blackthorn on the lane

and climbing the slow hill, striping the turf, its grey horse
racing a big sky.

Along the line of the fence, a ghost owl flies on silent wing
while the weasel creeps to her nest.

The weasel creeps to her nest without brushing a leaf
breathing its pinbone mess of pellet and fur.

Darkling beetles steady at rustle and hiss, wait
for the long yolk falling.

Along the line of the fence, the ghost owl flies to her nest,
early light tracing the edge of her wing in each direction.

Her ears pinpoint sound in delay; last night's start
and patter, her hunger, buried in the fall of rain.

She disappears from sight, leaving her silence
and a glimmer of wire.

In the hedge, something woven from air and tats of down
is staring, its flyblown carcass stirring as if waking.

Earth resumes its humming; celandine secures the verge.
On the hill, the horse stoops to graze.

Broadland Birds

by

E. L. TURNER

The first nestling Bittern seen in England for more than 40 years.

AMONGST the inner circle of naturalists and lovers of the countryside, Miss Turner's name has long been known, but it is only recently that the daily press has brought her to the notice of a world-wide public. Retiring, even for a naturalist, she has pursued her labour of love, of observation, of comparison, and of photography at Hickling, on the Farne Island and at Scolt Head, with an almost superhuman patience and endurance. When she accepted the onerous and lonely post of Watcher at the National Trust Island of Scolt Head on the Norfolk Coast, the press, with a certain sense of misplaced humour, dubbed her in consequence "The Woman Crusoe."

For the first time the history of her life as a naturalist is made known to the world and the results of some of her most important and truly remarkable discoveries are collected into book form. Miss Turner has an admirably lucid and simple style; a style that gives her place with writers such as Gilbert White and W. H. Hudson.

COUNTRY LIFE LIBRARY

OUT ON HER OWN

SKIPPER OF THE BROADS

Words: James Parry
Photography: Emma L. Turner

From a remote base in the marshlands of Norfolk, ornithologist Emma L. Turner pioneered bird photography and championed conservation in the relentlessly masculine environment of early twentieth-century natural history.

'Just what it is in the marshland that grips the imagination and casts a spell over its lovers, I do not know,' wrote Emma Turner in her 1924 book *Broadland Birds*. 'We none of us know. It is a land of wide windswept spaces and far-flung horizons; of mystic nights and great silences.' This compelling and lyrical image of a landscape seemingly defiant of normal parameters was worth seeking out in person, I decided. So, one warm and sultry June evening, I took myself to Hickling, the village in the Norfolk Broads with which Turner became so closely associated, in search of some of the magic that kept pulling her back there, year after year. Pestered by mosquitos and struggling to find anywhere remotely dry or comfortable to sit, at first I was dubious that I could ever succumb as she had. But slowly, brushed by the reeds, the sedges and the breeze off the water, I fell into the mesmeric rhythm of this very singular place. With a silky dusk encroaching, I watched a lone great crested grebe cautiously and sinuously weave its way along a dyke. As it passed just a few feet in front of me, I began to understand what it was that so captivated Turner about these marshes and their wildlife and, in turn, inspired her to undertake what no other woman had done before. Heavy raindrops started to fall, but the reedbeds were still bursting with the noisy chuntering of warblers and every so often a water rail would squeal in alarm. Marsh harriers were sailing past on their final hunting sorties of the day. I had brought Turner's book with me, and I sat down in the fading light to see what she might have to say about the onset of marshland darkness. 'But it is the night that is so full of mystery in this land of big spaces,' she declared. I thought of her, out here on her own, a century before me and in a world so different from today.

Turner's achievements are impressive by any standard: active for over thirty years in leading ornithological circles; secured the first ever photographs of rare and elusive birds at the nest; jointly discovered that the bittern was breeding again in Britain; wrote several books and illustrated them with her own images; published a raft of papers and articles about her observations; was awarded a gold medal by the Royal Photographic Society; was accepted as the first 'honorary lady member' of the British Ornithologists' Union; was one of the first women admitted as fellows of the Linnean Society; and was a seminal figure in early bird conservation measures in Norfolk on Scolt Head and here at Hickling, where an island in the middle of the broad still bears her name. How, and particularly as a woman, did Emma Turner attain so much and why is she not better known today?

I first encountered the work of Turner by chance, browsing the shelves of a bookshop in the Norfolk town of Burnham Market. My eyes fell on a faded green spine and the words 'Broadland Birds, E.L. Turner' in gold lettering. Inside, a skim of the foxed pages revealed stories of long-ago ornithological adventures on the Norfolk Broads, with extraordinary photographs of birds at the nest and of a seemingly halcyon landscape of reeds and water. One image particularly stood out, of a woman wearing a large Edwardian hat and peering through some sort of optical instrument while a man in tweed looked on. The faintly amusing caption – 'Alfred Nudd awaits his turn of the stereoscope' – simply served to underline the dated and 'lost world' character of the book. It was only when I got home and had the chance to look at the book more closely that I realised that Turner was the woman in the picture and that it was she who had taken the remarkable images of birds over a century before.

Like most other aspects of Victorian and Edwardian public life, the world of natural history was dominated by an often competitive male cadre of obsessively keen amateurs with ample time and money on their hands ('professional' naturalists being virtually unknown at the time). In the latter respect, at least, Turner fitted the frame. She came from a comfortable background in Kent and the assumption must be that she was sustained largely by an independent private income for the whole of her adult life – she never married, and beyond what would have been modest royalties on her various books, and perhaps the occasional speaking fee, there is no evidence of her undertaking regular paid employment. She was a member of the leisured classes, enjoying the various advantages such status conferred.

There, however, her conventionality ends. She later wrote how, in 1900, 'the need of an outdoor occupation led me to take up photography'. While this popular medium was accepted as an appropriate pastime for women of Turner's class, it was to portraiture and landscape subjects that most such lenses were directed. 'Pictorial photography bored me,' was her typically unequivocal verdict. It appears that she became interested in bird photography as a result of a chance encounter with Richard Kearton, who, with his brother Cherry, was in the vanguard of early wildlife photography and film-making, alongside other pioneers such as Reginald Badham Lodge and Oliver Pike. Where and when Turner bought her first camera, and how she learned to use it, are still unknown, but in the spring of 1902 she arrived in the Norfolk Broads in search of birds to photograph, admitting later that she 'scarcely knew one wader from another' back then.

Of course, Turner was not the only woman of her time with an interest in birds. From the 1880s onwards, female protagonists had led an increasingly high-profile campaign against the slaughter of birds – such as kingfishers, great crested grebes and egrets – to fuel the burgeoning demand from the fashion industry for bird feathers and other avian body parts. Amongst the agitators was Emily Williamson, who in 1889 had founded the Plumage League, a women-only group whose members pledged not to wear feathers (from most species of birds, at least) – prompting the magazine *Punch* to issue a famously withering comment, 'Not a very severe self-denying ordinance that, Ladies?' Yet a powerful movement was emerging and, two years later, Williamson joined forces with Eliza Phillips, who was running the similarly minded Fur and Feather League, to form the Society for the Protection of Birds, which opened its doors to men and by 1899 had 20,000 members. In 1904, two years after Turner made her first photographic expedition to the Broads, the fledgling conservation body was incorporated by royal charter with the Duchess of Portland as its first president.

Turner's own views on the progress of moves towards greater bird protection, and on the role played by organisations such as the (by now) Royal Society for the Protection of Birds, can be gleaned from comments in her books. She had seen first-hand how the depredations of hunters and egg collectors had decimated the populations of certain bird species in the Norfolk Broads, driving some to extinction and reducing others to only a handful of breeding pairs. Writing about the ruff and the bittern in *Broadland Birds*, she rejected claims that their disappearance was the result of drainage and habitat loss, declaring that there was 'no doubt that both these species owe their destruction to the wholesale and indiscriminate slaughter which was systematically carried out during the breeding season'. It was a bittern that formed the subject of some of Turner's most celebrated photographs when, in the summer of 1911, she and the White Slea Lodge estate gamekeeper Jim Vincent discovered a fledgling bird at Sutton Broad. The evocative images taken by Turner constituted the first conclusive proof that bitterns had bred in Britain once again after decades of absence, while also affirming the principle that scientific evidence need not depend solely on a dead specimen in the hand. The images also ultimately helped to secure her a gold medal from the Royal Photographic Society.

By this time Turner was a familiar – if somewhat quirky – figure on the Broads. From her base at Hickling, she went out on photographic forays along the dykes and through the reedbeds in search of birds such as the bearded tit, the grasshopper warbler and the water rail, often accompanied by local marshmen Alfred and Cubit Nudd. They helped to locate suitable locations for photography (usually the site of an accessible nest), carried cumbersome equipment and erected screens behind which Turner would secrete herself, camera at the ready (although almost nothing is known of the gear Turner used, she undoubtedly would have deployed a weighty plate camera and tripod). She later described how, on at least one occasion, she lay down on the ground covered in rotting vegetation by way of camouflage with just her lens peeping out. She was rewarded with an exceptionally close encounter with a snipe, which walked over her, probing for food. 'Once or twice I felt the slender bill gently prodding my cheek all over,' she wrote in *Broadland Birds*, 'and once it was thrust into my ear.' What Turner called 'the rubbish-heap method of photography' had been pioneered by the Kearton brothers and was soon superseded by what we now know as 'hides' but what Turner referred to as 'the hiding-tent'. She seems to have regarded its advent with mixed feelings, lamenting how it had 'wholly done away with the old intimacy which so often existed between the photographer and stray birds'. ⤜

THE AVOCET AT HOME

A SKEIN OF GEESE

Turner used various waterborne craft when in the Broads, the most important of which – a modest houseboat called *The Water-Rail*, named after the first marsh bird she ever photographed – was built to her own design. Launched in 1905, it proved too wide to pass through Ludham Bridge and had to be loaded onto a trolley and taken to Hickling Broad by road. There it was moored next to a small island on which Turner later had built a small hut in which she would develop her photographs. At one point, although it is not clear exactly when, this place became known as Miss Turner's Island, a name that it retains today. Summer season boat trips from the Norfolk Wildlife Trust reserve at Hickling carry visitors past the 'island' (actually a promontory today), sometimes pausing alongside for the guide to say something about the woman after whom it is named. Now heavily overgrown with scrub, the island looked rather more orderly in Turner's day, if contemporary photographs are anything to go by. Today it feels lost and forgotten, which might not be wholly inappropriate for the former abode of someone who so clearly enjoyed its solitude.

Out in the field for hours on end, day after day, in what were often difficult conditions – she writes of falling into ditches and of problems with equipment (misted lenses and the like) – Turner must have developed a close working relationship with the Nudds and other local people, amongst whom she lived for much of the year. She was a single woman of a certain age and class, doubtless with a corresponding contemporary sense of propriety and formality – even if these were things she necessarily had to set aside on occasion. The language she uses in her writing deploys the class distinctions of the day but also betrays a hint of wry, self-deprecatory humour. 'From both landowners and marshmen I have always received kindness and help,' she explains. 'At first the native population of Hickling looked upon me as a harmless lunatic… Now, after twenty years, they take me for granted, and even look upon me as one of their chief shows.' Despite what might be read as an enduring sense of 'them and us', it is clear that Turner respected and valued the affinity the local communities felt for their marshland environment and how the futures of both were inextricably linked and unique. 'They are a race apart, these Broadsmen,' she wrote. The social upheavals prompted by the First World War, with a greater prominence given to the role of women and a breakdown in traditional systems of class patronage and social hierarchy, would not have escaped Turner, even in the still remote communities of rural Norfolk. Yet there seems to be no evidence that, despite her success in making her way in what was overwhelmingly a man's world, she harboured any particular views on the cause of female equality, for example, or at least articulated them as such. What did she make of the suffragettes and their campaign for the enfranchisement of women? Overall, the emphasis in her writing is decidedly less on people than on birds (she writes rather dismissively of 'the public' on more than one occasion), although she understood perfectly how a more enlightened human engagement with the environment would be vital if birds were to be protected effectively and prosper.

A particular conservation cause célèbre that Turner tackled head on involved the colonies of terns nesting along the North Norfolk coast, specifically on the island of Scolt Head. By the early 1920s, the number of birds there was much diminished as a result of both egg collection (primarily by local villagers for their own consumption or sale) and disturbance, whether wilful or inadvertent. To help protect the terns, the island had been bought by the National Trust with funds raised by the Norfolk and Norwich Naturalists' Society, but a 'presence' was required on site during the breeding season to ensure that the birds were left unmolested. When no volunteers for the post of tern-watcher could be found, Turner put herself forward. Accommodation was basic – a hut with hardly any amenities to speak of – and supplies had to be brought over from the mainland. Undeterred, the fifty-seven-year-old doyenne of Hickling took up her post. 'I was only a stop-gap until a suitable man could be found,' she later wrote. In the event, she guarded the ternery for two seasons, in 1924 and 1925, a period that saw more than a doubling in the number of breeding pairs of common tern. Subsequently, she was succeeded by Charles Chestney, Scolt's first permanent warden.

Today, Scolt Head is managed by Natural England on behalf of the National Trust, and the hut that served as Turner's home for two consecutive summers is still there (although higher-spec accommodation has since been provided a short distance away for modern-day tern wardens). When I visited in September 2017, I found the original hut full of character and features that I have little doubt Turner would recognise, including the wooden sleeping cabins that she wrote about in *Bird Watching on Scolt Head* as nearly going up in flames when hot embers spewed out of the open fire and careered across the living area before she managed to sweep them up.

The resilience and adaptability shown by Turner during her time on Scolt Head confirmed her as capable and resourceful, seemingly happy to turn her own hand to practical jobs rather than seeking or awaiting assistance. Amongst the various vessels in the Turner flotilla at Hickling was *The Grey Plover*, on which she describes carrying out repairs herself: 'During the War, when labour was scarce, I knocked out half the inside fittings and re-built them to my own liking. *The Grey Plover* is not much to look at and perhaps unworthy of the name she bears; nevertheless she is something I love and my ultimate refuge from the strife of tongues.'

That Turner enjoyed her own company, away from idle chatter, is not in any doubt. Much was made by the Fleet Street press of her appointment as the Scolt Head tern-watcher in 1924 and the fact that she would be living on her own on an island only accessible when the tide and weather allowed. She deeply resented what she termed 'the myth of "The Loneliest Woman in England"' that was peddled by the media, and was at pains to point out that she 'was never lonely and seldom alone'. She was accompanied by her five dogs, for one thing. When visitors made it across to Scolt, as many did, whether invited friends, fellow naturalists or simply roving reporters after a story, they had to be prepared to muck in and take orders. A brusque welcome might be the best that could be hoped for by strangers, but there is evidence of Turner's bark being worse than her bite. After berating one party of arriving newsmen, she deployed them as her 'carriers', getting them to trudge across the saltings with her equipment and supplies. It was an episode that appeared to end well, however. 'They were cheerful and willing helpers,' she wrote, 'and entered into the fun of the journey. It was a beautiful April day and everything wore its most becoming smile.'

At this point Turner was well established as a leading, if rather unconventional, figure in the realms of both bird photography and ornithology. She had already published *The Home-Life of Some Marsh-Birds* (1907), plus a string of highly regarded articles (notably in the journal *British Birds* and in *Country Life*) on her ornithological records and field trips. Three important books were to follow, all published by *Country Life* and illustrated with her own pictures: *Broadland Birds* (1924) (which remains her best-known publication), *Bird Watching on Scolt Head* (1928) and *Stray Leaves from Nature's Notebook* (1929). She mixed with many of the leading natural historians of the day, including the legendary Arthur Patterson, and was on especially cordial terms with the Reverend M.C.H. Bird, an

A FLOCK OF SANDWICH TERNS

THE SALTINGS, SCOLT ISLAND, LOW TIDE

outstanding amateur naturalist dubbed 'the Gilbert White of the Broads'. Her suite of high-level connections is underlined by her friendship with the Duke and Duchess of Bedford, with whom she stayed on a visit to Scotland. Doubtless she would have used such contacts to try to advance what she saw as the cause of conservation; one particular bugbear was excessive development along Britain's coastline – 'the encroachment of villadom and bungalow towns', as she called it. She was equally energised by the need to raise funds so that conservation could be truly long term and sustainable: 'It is one thing to acquire these beauty spots… it is another thing to maintain them for the nation. Money, and yet more money, is needed.'

If the first decade of the twentieth century marked Turner's arrival on the photographic and ornithological stage (1904 saw her and fifteen other women proposed as fellows of the Linnean Society, the first of their gender to be admitted in that way), then the 1920s could be viewed as her time in the sun-filled uplands. Admired and respected by her peers, she had become a leading figure in the British ornithological establishment, the first woman to do so and by sheer dint of her hard work, professionalism and dedication. Ten years later, and with her photography days over, her life had changed rather dramatically. She had moved to Cambridge, where she enjoyed tending her garden and worked hard to finish her final book, *Every Garden a Bird Sanctuary* (1935). Tragedy was to strike in the form of a bungled eye operation that saw her lose her sight. Undaunted, she continued her membership of the Cambridge Bird Club (which she had helped to found in 1925), enjoying occasional field trips and especially visits to her home by the younger members, whom she would ask to read aloud to her from the latest ornithological journals. They would affectionately call her 'Skipper', a reference to her watery days on the Broads.

I find this image of Turner surrounded by enthusiastic young birders especially telling. It is tempting to conclude from her time spent on the island at Hickling Broad and out on Scolt Head that she was something of a recluse and sought out such isolated locations in a quest for solitude. But this would not be even a remotely accurate reading of the situation. She was not there so much for herself as for the birds that she so loved, and it is clear from her books and correspondence that she received regular (sometimes extended) visits from friends and acquaintances in both places. She doubtlessly enjoyed the peace and quiet of Hickling, Scolt and elsewhere, and certainly does not appear to have suffered fools gladly, but she was also sociable and generous with her time, especially when amongst people with whom she shared a passion for wildlife and the outdoors.

Emma Turner died in August 1940. In addition to confirming her attainment of 'a foremost place in the ranks of ornithologists', the obituaries spoke of her enthusiasm, kindliness, sense of humour, perseverance, vitality and courage, 'and above all the friendly hand she had for all her fellow bird-lovers'. Sadly, what must have been a formidable archive of her original photographic material has never been found and is presumed lost. Its disappearance perhaps explains, at least in part, why Turner faded from view in the decades after her death.

Piecing together a more complete panorama of Turner's imagery beyond what was published in her books has relied largely on detective work in journal archives and on chance discoveries, the most significant of which came in 2011 as a result of an article I wrote in the Norfolk Wildlife Trust newsletter, *Tern*. In response to seeing the feature, Alison Horne, the great-grand-daughter of the Reverend M.C.H. Bird, contacted me to say that she had found a series of photographs in the Bird family archive that she believed to be by Turner, as well as a series of letters exchanged between the two. Some of the images in question are definitely Turner's, and others very probably so. The letters, meanwhile, are a remarkable resource and have shed valuable light on two of the leading figures in early twentieth-century Norfolk natural history circles. Contact with Joan Keeling and Julia Volrath, both great-nieces of Turner with personal and family memories of 'Aunt Emma', has also helped to fill in some of the gaps in our understanding of the remarkable life and achievements of this pioneer of wildlife photography.

A REED WARBLER RETURNS TO ITS NEST

STAR OF THE SEA

ON URCHINS AND ANCIENT WATERS

Words: Alex Woodcock
Illustration: Lucy Eldridge

Fossilised sea urchins, or echinoids, are regular finds in the chalk-rich counties of the south of England. Etched with a distinctive five-pointed star pattern, they have been collected for millennia and set in doorways, windows and burial mounds to shine a light into the unknown.

'There's no easy way of getting there,' says my friend Simon as he throws the car down yet another narrow lane fringed with runoff streams. It's a Friday at the end of January and the land is wet and heavy with the last grip of winter, though we have chosen a spectacular day to head out to this forgotten corner of Hampshire – the roads are almost blinding in the sun. Skeletal trees and patches of snowdrops gather at the edges before giving way to the chalky mud of fields and, above, red kites draw circles in the blue. When we stop, the quietness is like a silent roar.

Sea urchins are the reason we are out here. Dead ones, dead for millions of years, creatures that lived in long-gone and unnamed seas and now remaining only as fossil impressions. I'd read that fossil urchins, or echinoids

(from the Greek *echinos*, a hedgehog, for in life they are covered with prickly spines), had been set above one of the windows of St Peter's church at Linkenholt, framing the top of the arch of a window. This pairing of gothic architecture and ancient fossil had intrigued me, sparking a dormant memory about the fossils here being considered lucky, though just where I'd picked up this information I couldn't remember. The fossils were flint casts of the urchins' rounded bodies, each one preserving the characteristic star pattern on the top of the shell. In the photograph I'd seen, the fossils were placed so that this naturally occurring star was visible. No doubt, the star was the reason for their esteemed position in the church, where to some degree they mimicked earlier stone-carving designs – the geometric shapes beloved by the Romanesque masons spring to mind. But the more I looked into it the more I found a whole host of other associations and uses going back into the distant past, and these few above the window at St Peter's church were just one example of the centuries-long fascination that we've had with these fossil stars.

While there are many different types of ancient urchin, the ones most often found as fossils in the chalk are the oval-bodied (and from the side slightly pyramidal) *Echinocorys*, the more spherical *Conulus* and the heart-shaped *Micraster*. Their life on the sea bed predisposed them in death to being buried and fossilised, and it is perhaps for this reason that their remains are abundant today. Swimming above them in this long-gone ocean of the Cretaceous period would have been other recognisable creatures such as sharks and plesiosaurs. Incredible as it is to think, these fossils connect us with an era before the great extinction of the dinosaurs – they are a bridge across time.

The land rises and falls as we pursue ever narrower roads. We are trailing the edges of counties, criss-crossing between Hampshire and Wiltshire, following where the gentle chalk slopes cede into coombes sheltering nests of trees, on roads that zigzag around old field boundaries or cling to the sky along the tops of hills. Long barrows and solitary, abandoned stones chart our progress. Everywhere there is mud, pale where it has been cut by the plough, darker at the edges of the road where it has mingled with old leaves and other organic matter. A field is picked over by an assorted mix of rooks and crows, flints and feathers glinting blue-black in the damp air.

It was a few weeks ago, in the Sussex Archaeological Society library in Lewes, that I found a paper called 'Shepherds' Crowns in Archaeology and Folklore'. It was written by Herbert Samuel Toms, the curator of the Brighton Museum from 1896 to 1939 and a former student of archaeological pioneer Augustus Pitt Rivers. The day was a rainy one and it was a pleasure to sit in the small book-lined room of the library, which looked out over the rooftops of Lewes to the velvet of the downs beyond.

Following the death of his wife Christina in 1927, Toms took to long walks through the countryside. If these were contemplative then they were also data-gathering exercises, with Toms collecting and recording local lore. I started at the back of the piece and so came across Toms' catalogue of names for the fossil echinoids first: shepherds' crowns, shepherds' hats, policemen's helmets, fairy heads, fairy loaves, fairy weights, shepherds' hearts, knee-caps, beggar-man's knees, bishop's knees, shepherds' knees, lucky stones and thunderstones. The names, with the place or places of collection noted for each – fairy weights on the Isle of Wight, fairy heads in Cerne Abbas, for example – seemed vaguely nonsensical, otherworldly and entirely logical: perfect descriptions of the stones themselves.

In his short paper, Toms gathered together a wealth of information, all of which revealed a use of these fossils in times of loss and threat, from grave goods in prehistoric burials to amulets (particularly favoured by nineteenth-century shepherds) worn or carried to prevent being struck by lightning. Their inclusion in burials was by no means unusual, occurring in ones and twos at the Neolithic camp at Whitehawk near Brighton, and sometimes in their hundreds, as at Dunstable Down in Bedfordshire. Here the Bronze Age interment of a young woman and child was found within a circle of echinoid fossils, in places as many as three deep, their skeletons at the centre of a perfect halo of protective stones.

There was one paragraph that particularly intrigued me as I'd never heard of such a thing before. It concerned what Toms understood as a 'mound of remembrance'. One of these, the tumulus at Poiron, Deux-Sèvres, in Poitou, west-central France, he went on to describe:

> *The mound, twenty metres in diameter, was enclosed by a circular earthen embankment. Its excavation revealed neither burial, trace of metal, stone tools, nor charcoal, and it was formed of local schistose stones – a kind of cairn. At the centre five flat slabs of schist formed a sort of quadrangular box, similar to the niche or cavity seen in pigeon-houses; and, in the centre of this niche or recess was found a solitary fossil sea-urchin placed on a flat slab of schist. No sea-urchin fossil occurred in the district.*

A mound at the centre of which there was a fossil echinoid? In the darkness of the earth, a buried star. It sounded like something from a novel or a folktale. The image of that mound and its solitary, boxed urchin hung in my mind for days, broadcasting its power across the centuries as if through an infinity mirror. The more I thought about it, the more I felt something below the surface of everyday life move, my thoughts stirring the dead magic that it held. I wanted to find out more.

'We're here,' says Simon, as we pull up beside a Victorian church backed with a stand of trees. From the car I can see the fossils arranged around the window.

Flint is everywhere in these southern counties: fields are full of it, big spherical nodes chipped or split by the plough. Further to the east, where the chalk meets the sea, it strikes charcoal lines through the cliffs before weathering out to form beaches of grey pebbles. But its ubiquity cloaks what is, on closer looking, an unusual stone.

Flint is a pseudomorph, a secondary or 'false-formed' rock. This means it is a rock that has been deposited in the place of another kind of rock, which has been dissolved away. So the echinoids around the window of St Peter's church are casts – the shape of the original fossil urchin now remembered in flint. Each one is the shape of absence, a twice-removed thing: like making a mould in which to cast something (say, plaster), casting it and then slowly replacing the plaster cast with another material. If this last step sounds extraordinary then it is. A complete transformation of matter over millions of years, from white calcium carbonate to black silica.

Gather enough absences together and a different territory emerges, one in which space is taken up at the same time as it's cancelled out. I felt this at a recent Rachel Whiteread exhibition at Tate Britain in London. Here her casts in various materials of everyday and unexceptional spaces, from the interior of a wardrobe to the air beneath chairs, seemed the physical equivalents of a faulty strip-light flickering in a strange luminescence of its own, neither fully on nor fully off. The casts themselves, acts of remembrance for spaces known but ignored, carried a sense of the monumental. Like a monument might make us stop and reflect, they caused a similarly reverential hush in the room, people moving quietly and speaking softly around them. I wondered whether this wasn't because, in some way, they mirrored our own absences, lighting up the dark and abandoned places. So too the flint urchins, casts of casts, heavy with liminal energy. Things of the deep past that have crossed into the present via geological processes that themselves border on the magical. Perfect, then, to find on a church, itself a space between the known and unknown. Above the window, twenty-five of them. Weathered to pale grey but nonetheless unmistakable, each one etched with its five-pointed star.

The church door was locked so I wandered around outside. On the other side there was a smaller window topped with more echinoids. The entire church had been rebuilt in the 1870s along with the neighbouring school (which features a window with yet more fossils), but it has been suggested that these urchins came from the earlier medieval church that no longer remains. The implication is that they were considered too important to leave behind so were incorporated into the new structure.

Certainly, the archaeology and folklore of these fossils is compelling. The prehistoric burials and remembrance mounds suggest our ancestors accorded the stones great significance. A star in the darkness of the earth might have been a light to guide the deceased to the next world, through the dangerous gap that later cultures would populate with monsters, its shape enough to bring some kind of comfort to both the living and the dead. As an apotropaic device, able to ward off harm, it brought protection, a sense of which lingered on in the local lore that Toms collected about these 'lucky stones'. In the Iron Age they were worn as amulets, and at a Gallo-Roman temple at Essarts in France they were found deposited with other votives including fossil ammonites, stone axes and a statuette of Venus. Anglo-Saxon burials sometimes continued the ancient practice of including an echinoid with the deceased. In one, at Westgarth Gardens, Bury St Edmunds, in Suffolk, the skeleton of a woman was found clutching a fossil *Echinocorys* in her right hand.

'Who could have thought of lending the elasticity of wings to an avalanche?' wrote the poet André Breton in *Arcane 17*, watching the great concentration of sea birds living on the Percé Rock off the coast of Quebec. I've recently been reading this mystical book, written during the 1940s in the shadow of this limestone giant that looms out of the sea, and his words come back to me now as I watch a red kite circling above the church and its attendant trees. Breton was making the point that the birds and the rock shared a connection, one beyond the rock simply being a convenient place to live. And here, it's true: feather and flint are connected. Flint is a mixed form of silica, containing varieties of other silica minerals such as quartz and opal. Opal, a much softer form, occurs elsewhere in nature, in the glossy straws of cereals and grasses, as well as in the feathers of some species of birds. So to some degree, then, wing and rock *are* one – flint and opal and feather and fossil urchin, all strangely linked by silica and millennia.

A few weeks later I'm in the research room of the Brighton Museum, where waiting for me are two desks each with tantalising shapes lying beneath layers of protective tissue paper. I tuck myself in beneath the nose of a plaster-cast greyhound and behind the terracotta finial of a dragon, as Dan, the curator of local history and archaeology who has prepared these wonders in advance of my visit, removes the paper and talks me through what they are. On one desk there are books, on the other a selection of holed stones and echinoid fossils from various locations, all meticulously catalogued by Toms. The highlight of the selected books, collected cuttings and papers is a small album of his photographs, complete with meticulous notes on when and where they were taken, recording urchin fossils, holed stones and horseshoes displayed around the doorways and windows of houses in Sussex and Dorset.

It's an unusually engrossing read, both for the folklore recorded from the owners or tenants of each property and for their relationship to the fossils, as well as for Toms' detailed remarks. For example, on page 7:

> *SHEPHERDS CROWNS*
> *(2) Photographed 9th June, 1929,*
> *1.30pm., f32, 1/5sec.*
> *Mr E. Ansell, 171, Clapham Street,*
> *Clapham, nr Worthing*
>
> *I first saw these crowns when the Ansells were occupying the Whitmarsh cottage, Arundel Road, Clapham, 14th April, 1929, where Ansell then lived with his father-in-law, Mr Henry Field. His wife, Field's daughter, said they regarded the crowns as curios, but some years ago her father had sold two crowns to a young couple. Sometime after this young couple returned and gave Field an additional ten shillings because the crowns had brought them luck.*

The accompanying photograph shows a small window along the base of which, on the brick-width sill, are ten roughly equally sized and spaced near-perfect fossil urchins. I'm not surprised to learn that echinoid fossils of this quality were being traded in the 1920s; if the ones bought by the young couple had matched the ones in the photograph then I'd have paid for them too, regardless of any associated folklore.

I have a fossil echinoid, a *Micraster*, found in recent weeks near Cow Gap at the Eastbourne end of the South Downs. In comparison to these examples it is tiny, heavily weathered and missing two limbs of its star pattern, wearing the disguise of a nondescript pebble – because of this, it is an amazing find. I had found a website about local geology that suggested that some of the beaches along the Sussex coast were good fossil locations. Littlehampton to the west was one, but the general drift of the tide from west to east, and the fact that the fossils fall out of the cliffs with some regularity, suggested that anywhere along this stretch of coast might yield a find.

It was low tide and the sea turquoise blue when I set out with a friend, Louise, to look. The white tips of the waves were breaking over the white chalk rocks and making a perfect transition from water to stone, which, if you looked at it long enough, suggested that the stone itself was moving. It's a topsy-turvy thought, the interchangeability of stone and sea, but then the shimmering cliffs behind us were once the seabed and the urchin fossils themselves are relics of long-dead oceans. In a place of overlap such as this, everything seems to have come from something else.

We set to work, with only vague ideas of what size pebble to look for and what part of the beach to scour. I wondered how our ancestors had gone about looking for them. Were they sought out on special occasions, for example when someone had died, in order to place with them in death – like the hundreds found at Dunstable – or were they stockpiled and saved for such occasions? Were some locations deemed significant simply because of their presence? These and other thoughts flew around my mind as I crouched amongst the pebbles and milky rockpools, turning stones over, trying to get my eye into the size and shape of stone that might present a star.

After nearly two hours of looking, Louise was the first to turn over a tiny fossil. It wasn't even two inches long but carried a delicate star on one side – a *Micraster* urchin, beaten by the tide but nevertheless distinct. I soon turned up another, three arms of its star marked out by parallel lines of white dots, the other two weathered back to a single hollow. The fossils were so small and easy to miss I still can't quite believe we found them.

Waiting for the train home, I realise that I have my prize with me. Not on purpose – it's just found a home in my coat pocket and I've left it there, no doubt hoping to attract some luck. Turning it over in my hand, I think of Toms wandering through the countryside in the 1920s and of all of the people who've collected these fossils, stretching back through the centuries. They seem inconsequential things to have inspired so much interest.

On the train I place the *Micraster* on the empty table in front of me. Perhaps the star tattoo on these fossils isn't so much an abstract design of something out there, in space, a light shining through the emptiness, as it is a living thread that connects people across the generations. This is shape as remembrance, not only of pre-human landscapes and lifeforms but also of those who have lived before. The train fills up at Lewes and, as I am joined at my table by others, I slip the fossil back into my pocket. I don't want to lose it but neither do I want it to attract any attention. With this thought I realise I'm being drawn into their secret world, that I too am now an acolyte of these mysterious stones and indeed, on some level, a carrier of their lore.

The old beliefs die slowly – I can understand that. Perhaps at some unimaginable point in the future these fossils will all have been weathered back to amorphous lumps of grey flint, stripped of their markings. But until that time they will continue in their long afterlife, lending shape and meaning to the lives of others and protecting them from the dangers of the unknown. They are archives of ancient water, they are memories from before the time of memory. I can happily subscribe to their enduring power.

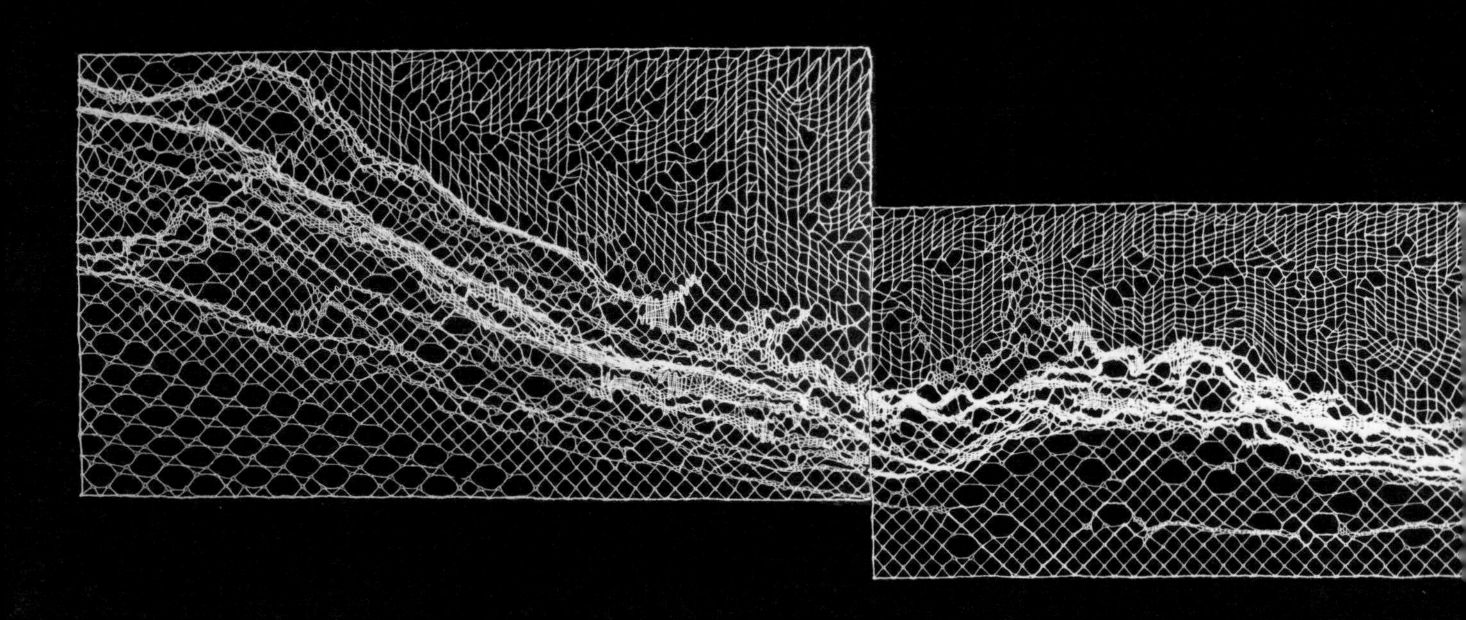

SEABLEED

TRANSLATING A SHIFTING TERRAIN INTO LACE

Words: Jane Atkinson
Photography: Peter Smith & Jay Armstrong

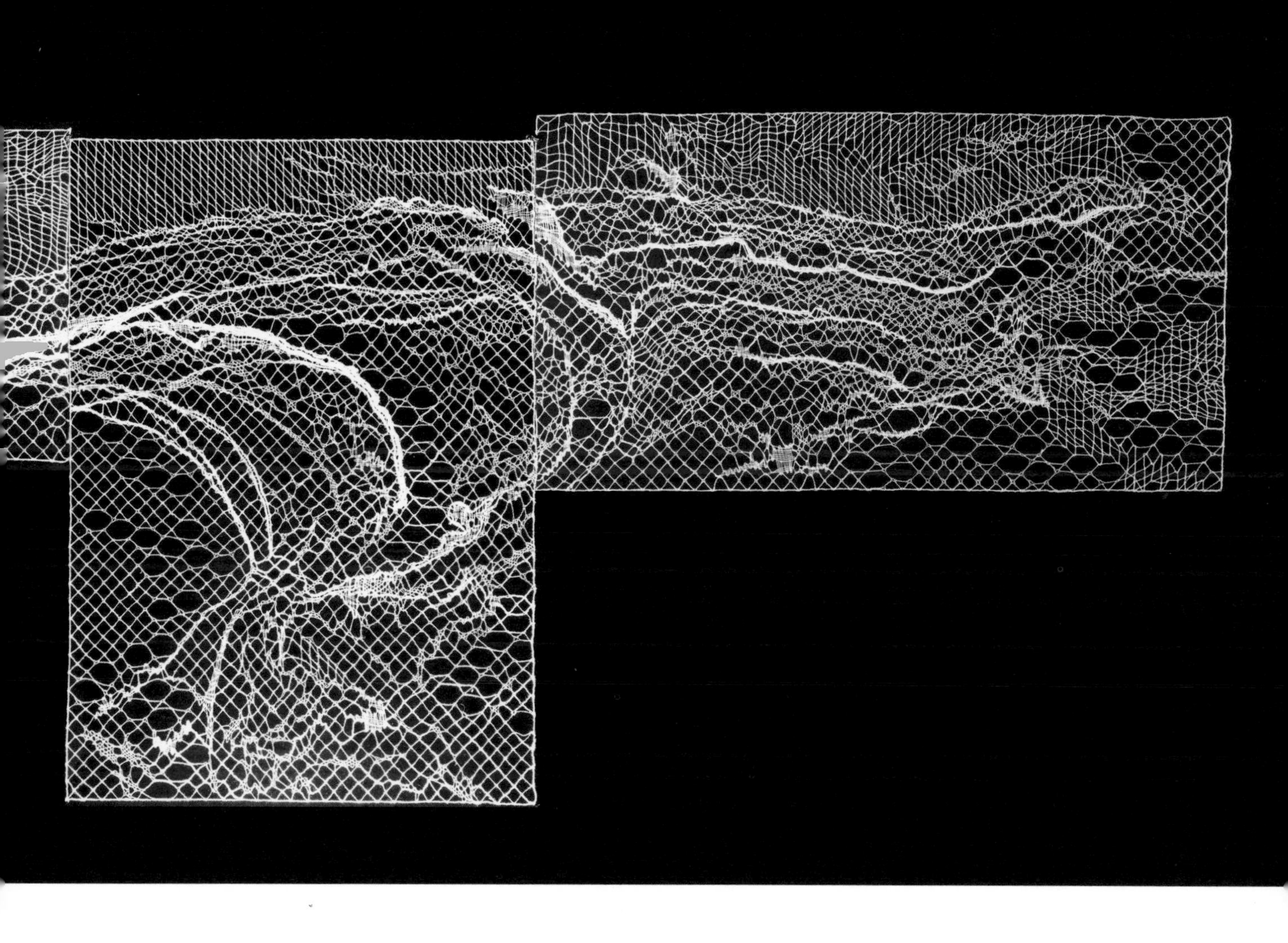

Inspired by a daily walk on Stanpit Marsh near her home in Dorset, a lacemaker seeks to convey in thread the delicate formations made by tidal swirls and eddies. It requires ingenuity and a life's experience to weave a panel of lace that speaks of the fragility of a shifting landscape.

I need to wind more bobbins with thread. There are already about 250 on my lace pillow, but I've reached a point where I could do with more. I'm not following a traditional pricking – instead I take my lead from a sweeping festoon of pattern I saw floating on the marsh some time ago, which I've sketched on board and laminated. I'm having to draw on all my years of making to translate what I saw into a panel of contemporary lace. I walk the marsh most days, but in thirty-five years I'd never seen anything like this. The surface of the water was charged with fine threads of what looked like thin white paint bleeding out from rotting seaweed. The wind swirled it into undulating gauzy tresses, diaphanous ribbons hair-fine and densely textured. I have seen other arresting conformations on these salt pans – etiolated clouds of bubbles, eddying traceries of dust. Frequent visits over several decades have built memories to which I have added a photo diary – but this is new.

The philosopher Friedrich Nietzsche detected something he named 'eternal recurrence', where an anticipated view creates a resonance shared by both the landscape and the returning walker. Many others, including Aristotle, have walked the same path every day, finding solace and renewal, a space to think. Each day I take the same route but, on the marsh, yesterday's land could be today's water. My walk crosses different terrain depending on the state of the tides and moods in the weather – parts of my route are intermittently submerged as the waters rise and fall. This piece of land is in daily conversation with salt water – here in Christchurch Harbour we have double tides, as does much of the south coast of England, due to the bottleneck effect of the Dover Strait. ➳

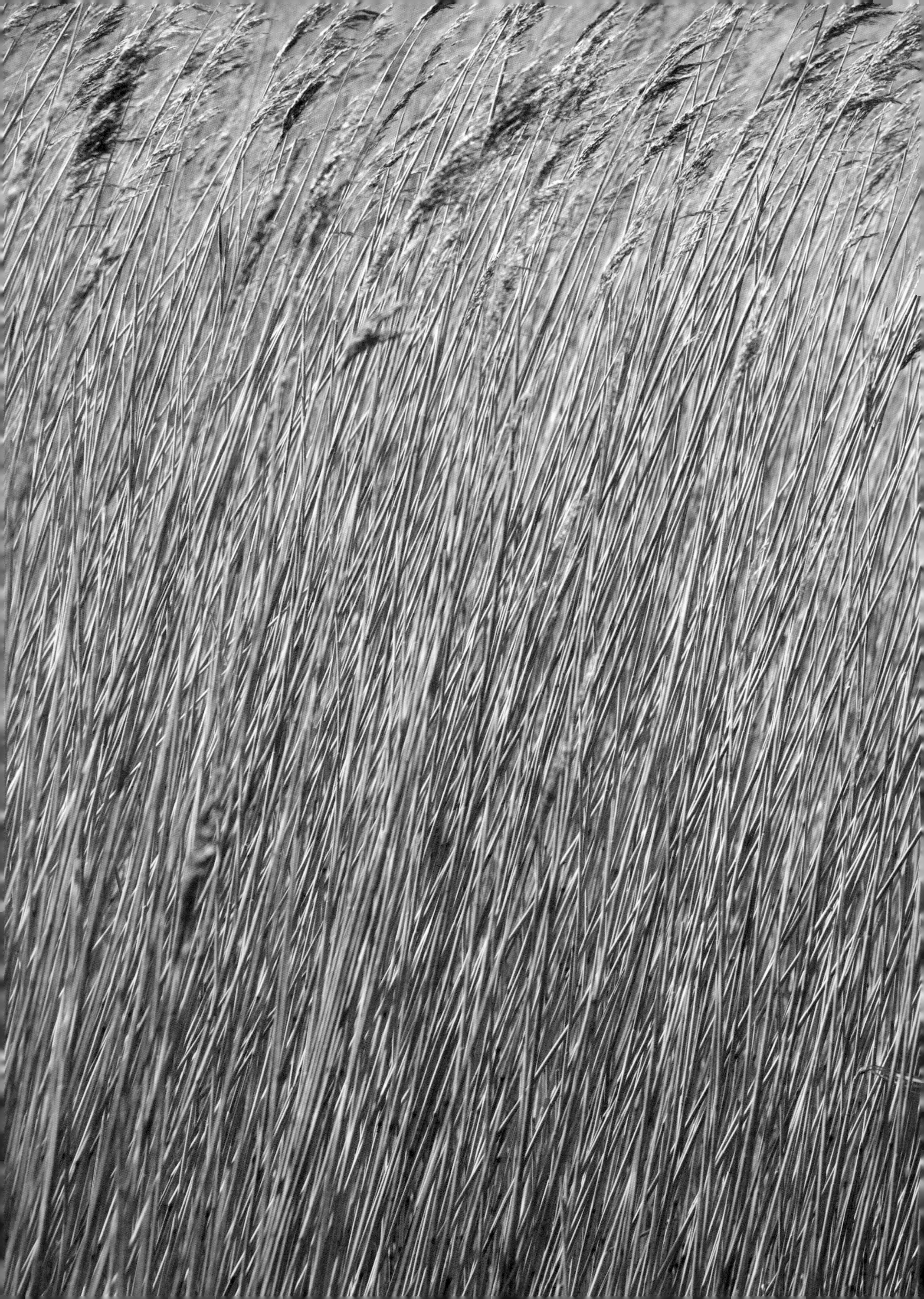

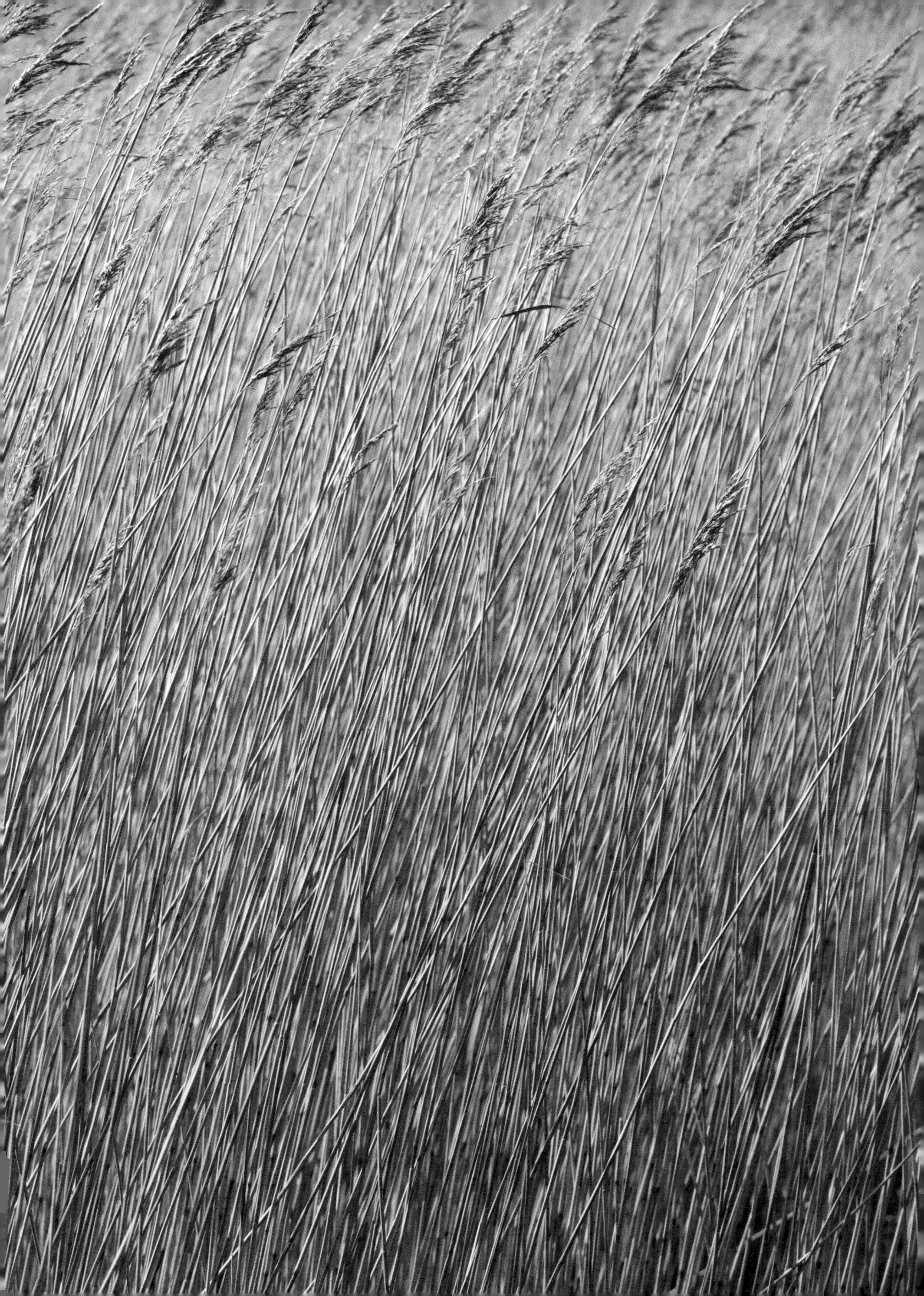

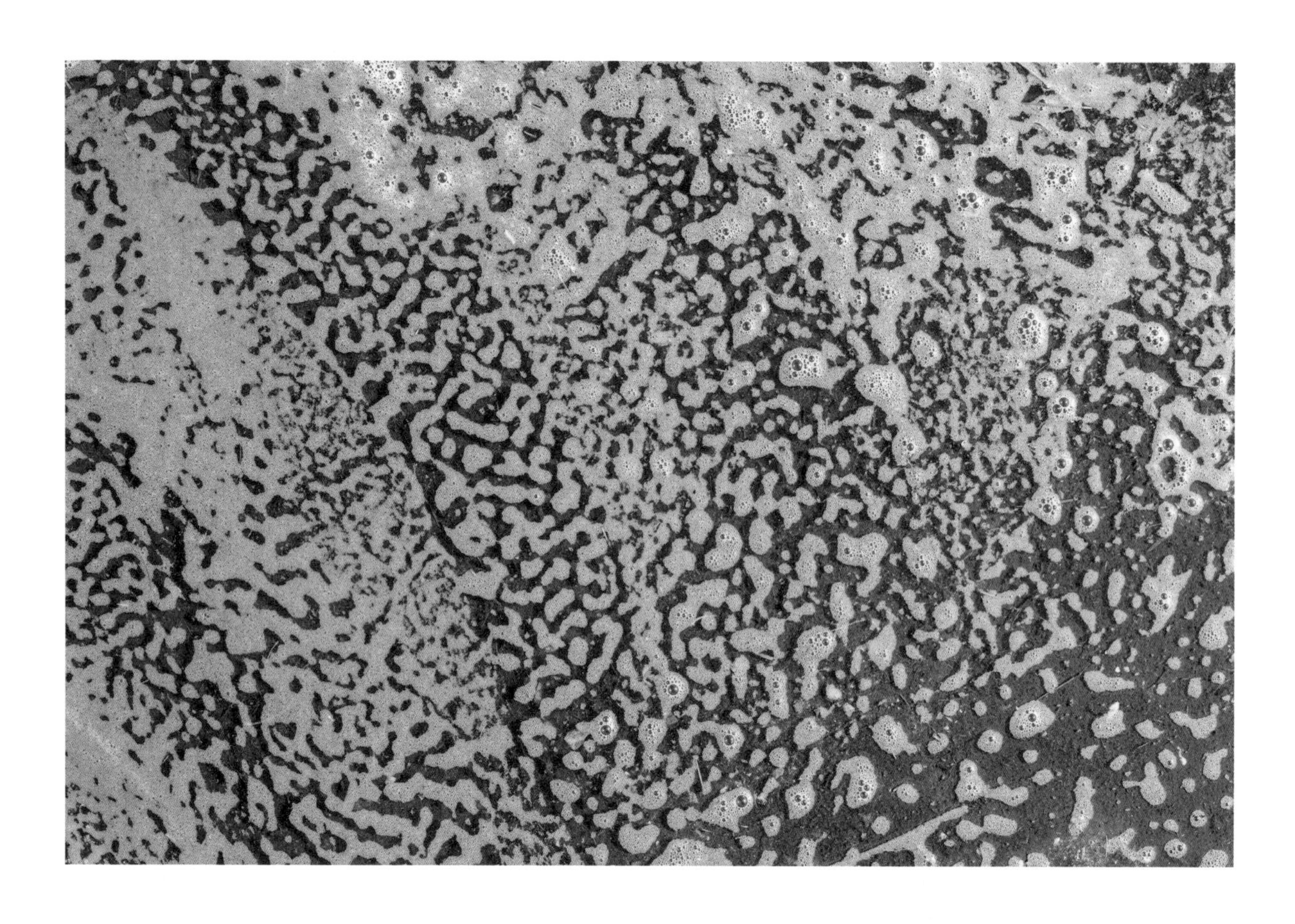

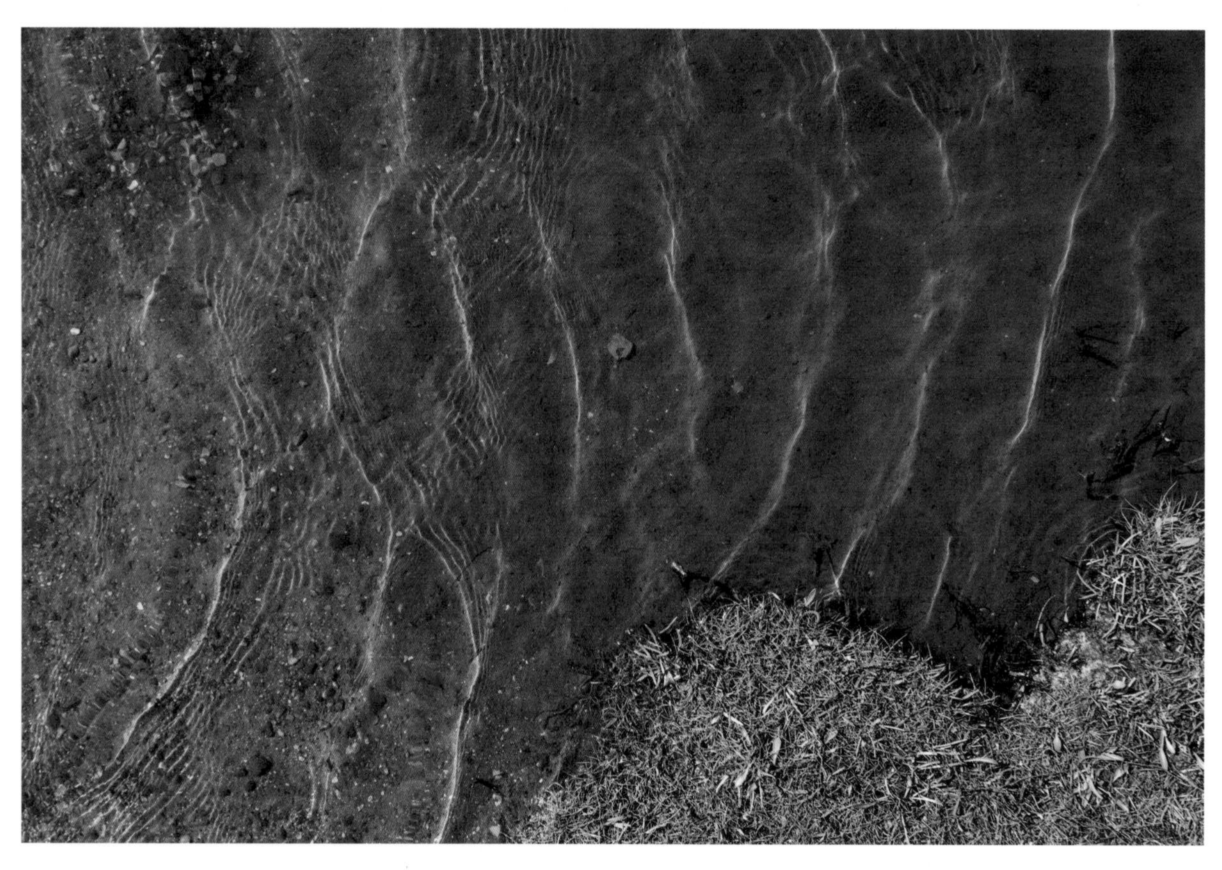

Crossing through a gate from suburbia, the first view is of a low sward interlaced with pools and runnels – minute differences in the height of the water that fills them tell me how difficult the path may be to traverse further on. This part of the path is a causeway that runs beside a higher level of ground that is mainly used by dog walkers. It also rolls with dips and bumps – previous generations thought landfill would deliver municipal buildings and playing fields, but the underlying landscape reasserted itself like the pea beneath the princess.

Past the poplar and willow windbreak at the end (sadly snaggle-toothed since around a third blew down in this decade's storms), and the rest of the marsh opens out. There are mudflats where migrant birds feed and roost, and low vegetation – swathes of reeds and rushes – is patrolled by grazing ponies. The path leads down to the confluence of the Dorset Stour and the Hampshire Avon rivers, which flow into Christchurch Harbour. Between the marsh and this natural harbour is Grimmery Bank, a spine of high ground that lies between the water and the land.

Crouch Hill in front of me crouches higher than its surroundings, surmounted by the wreck of a Beaker barrow abandoned by the archaeologists who bore off the Bronze Age burial to the local museum. At times, the waters rise to cover the whole marsh, but never this feature. A Bronze Age causeway – built when the sea was lower and further away – leads to the hill, where seven-thousand-year-old flints found in the sand bear the percussion marks of Mesolithic knapping. There I found another type of stone, one with a crazed pattern on its grey surface. I learned that these were Stone Age cooking stones, which would have been baked in a fire and then dropped scalding hot into a container of cold water to boil. Once, from a more recent age, I also found round shot possibly used for wildfowling or smuggling. The people who occupied this area over millennia past lived from what land and sea delivered.

The pools along the path have fuelled my lace experiments, offering beautiful air pockets contoured beneath iridescent ice crystals with sunlight glinting off the surface or refracted beneath it in golden 'caustic' ripples. I translate these into panels and hangings. Traditionally, lace is carefully plotted on rigid grids, but the marsh has inspired me to try fluid grids and extempore interpretation. Tristan Gooley, in his book *How to Read Water*, explains the factors that determine ripple shape and frequency – how they reflect, refract, diffract. I'm fascinated that people in cultures other than my own read water – I've been trying for years.

But subtle changes during recent decades have overtaken me. Thick ice is rare now, and spectacular crystals seldom get the several days of freezing weather they need to develop. Down by the river at Grimmery Bank, where I found the convolution from which I'm now working, the water is warming so much in summer that new seaweeds are taking hold. I suspect the one I saw rotting that day was the Pacific red seaweed *Gracilaria vermiculophylla*, brought into the harbour by visiting leisure craft last summer. It stank out the village when it died off in the autumn – I had never smelled anything like it. Thick mats of weed covering the mudflats prevent small waders from feeding, and rotting weed removes the oxygen from the water that other species need. It is also a pollution indicator.

Whereas I once walked year-long in shoes, I now need boots throughout the winter and on spring tides. Liquid incursions once merely inconvenient have had to be surmounted with ever-more-substantial boardwalks. Projections show we are lucky still to be walking here – the next generation will lose the opportunity as sea levels rise ever faster. Eastern philosophy reminds us that everything is impermanent, but we don't seem to be registering clearly enough just how fragile our landscape is. Apparently, something as inconsequential as the temperature of the room in which we read climate-change statistics affects how seriously we take them. If everything appears normal, we can be tempted to disregard the evidence.

Other walkers pass unheeding as I crouch with my camera, attempting to capture this delicate moment – often shifting, disappearing even as I press the button. I later ponder its significance as I preserve its shape in thread. Back towards the edge of the marsh, as I make my way home along another causeway, reputedly built to train First World War soldiers to practise hauling artillery across Flanders mud, I pass the pool that inspired my most adventurous set of lace panels. It held a huge pattern of bubbles, likely to be oxygen and nitrogen, sent up by the encroaching tide from roots in already waterlogged, oxygen-poor soil.

The landfilled recreation ground I cross at the end of my walk is breathing methane, eighty-six times more toxic for global warming than carbon dioxide. Salt marsh is now recognised as a carbon sink, locking carbon away for thousands of years (look at the way sodden artefacts in the Fens have lasted since the Bronze Age). If we had let well alone, we might have been in a better state now, for when we drain wetlands we release all that stored carbon as well as denying the planet the extra blessing of lush plant growth that sequesters carbon from the air. Friends of the Earth calls the five thousand coastal landfill sites around the UK a 'ticking time bomb', and these sites will need to be protected as the sea rises. The fly ash under my feet (generated from the chimneys of thousands of local houses and dumped on bare ground with no liner) could contain around eighteen heavy metals, including arsenic, which is toxic to humans and no doubt to the fish in the river and the mud-dwelling invertebrates on which the birds feed. ⤚

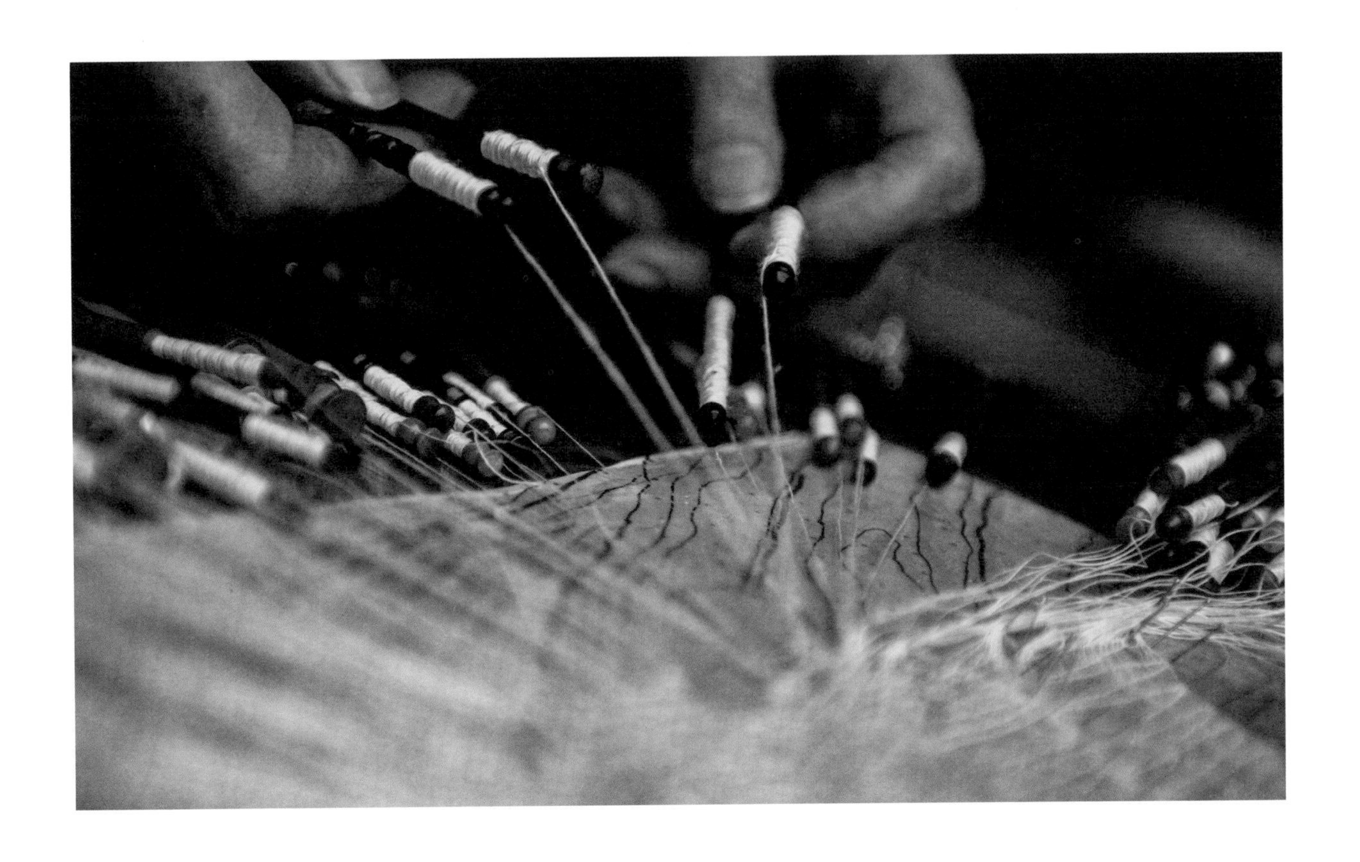

By selecting images to turn into lace that capture visual evidence of climate breakdown, I am creating conversation pieces that make it more real, both for me and I hope for the audience at my exhibitions. I am now discovering that my lace pieces can take this discussion public. That is, if I can manage to complete them – and it may be that I can't with this pattern, that I've reached the edge of my capabilities, this being the piece that finally takes me out of my depth. On this piece, there are times when I can only work for a short period before I face an impasse, when I get the unbearable urge to do the ironing, to back off, when my brain hurts with effort. Winding new thread onto old bobbins shifts the pressure to another day.

These patterns take me away from my roots in traditional fine lacemaking but back towards them, too. I've always tested the margins of what it's possible to construct, imagining designs into which I could weave the most air, finding the limits of the medium and of myself. At one point, I was making the largest pieces of lace I could manage as quickly as possible – banners, wall hangings, scarves – in threads the weight of four-ply knitting wool, thick enough to wind onto bobbins the size of pepper mills. Now I am allowing myself to linger over panels of detailed work in fine threads again, still spread over a wide area but suitable for the resurrection of my Victorian bobbins.

Working from Stanpit Marsh has set physical boundaries that have enabled me to push the limits of my lacemaking and free up my creativity. They have also given me independence and identity as a maker. For years I walked past a succession of fragile, remarkably lace-like formations but was baffled as to how to capture them in thread. One day I decided that I would find out somehow, and if I failed I would simply keep trying. Maybe age has something to do with it. I have lived here since I was thirty, and I have been walking the marsh daily since I was fifty. Reaching sixty, I had published several decades' worth of experiments on turning lace into an art form – but then what? Standing at the funeral of a much-loved contemporary, wishing we had both achieved our individual dreams, I wondered what I had to lose by pushing for mine, into unknown territory. The marsh had inspired me for years and there was nowhere I knew better – perhaps it could draw me further?

The first few inches of 'Seableed', my response to the pattern I saw floating on the marsh water last summer, now cover my lace pillow. It might look impossibly complicated, but it's more straightforward than you think. Using four bobbins at a time, a pair in each hand, the lacemaker uses a binary system – think plain and purl in knitting, or 1 and 0 in computer code. With lace it is 'half-stitch' and 'whole-stitch'. Everything is a combination of these two things. For whole-stitch, you cross the two centre bobbins, left over right, then twist the left-hand and right-hand pairs right over left, then cross the centre bobbins again. This weaves the two pairs of threads through each other. Half-stitch leaves out the last movement.

Pins anchor the work in place as I weave and twist my way over a pattern. In most lace I know exactly what I am doing – it gets more difficult when I make it up as I go along, creating what is known as 'free lace'. I am following the shapes suggested by the pool, keeping an eye on my photo for clues on what to do next. My problem comes at the point when the wind snags the swirling pattern and I suddenly need to change direction or magic up more threads. I like being confronted with problems that force me to invent, refresh or research new methods. I would not miss this for the world.

There are points when I truly do not know what to do next. I identify with descriptions of cavers hanging over a dark hole on a length of rope and I can liken it to mountaineering, where you might edge along a precipice before your ledge peters out and you must retreat – I spent half of yesterday going backwards. I don't aspire to climb Everest, but casting assorted fears aside at my lace pillow – doggedly pressing forward, evaluating, retreating, trying again – has opened up more new opportunities than I could have imagined. This is lace unlike anything I have done before. I am learning so much, yet all that matters is the present moment – for, as I nudge sixty-eight, the future is always uncertain.

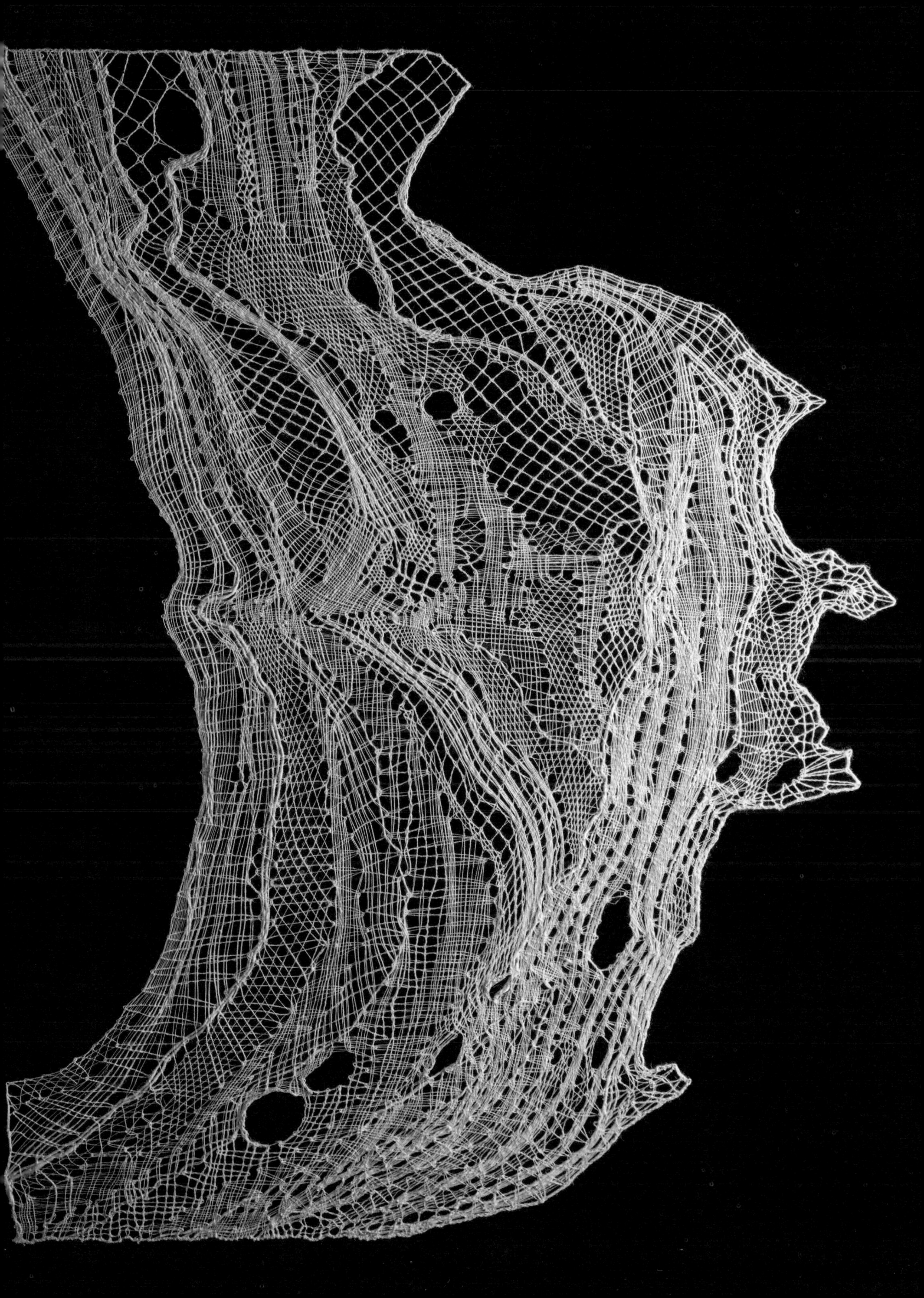

The work is confronting me with essential questions – above all, questions concerning my personal quest for 'eternal recurrence'. My local inspiration has always been ephemeral, but now it is in retreat. Sadly, this includes trees I have studied for foliar hangings and also birds – some populations, such as dunlin and ringed plover, have declined on the marsh by three quarters over the past twenty years. My lace allows me to confront people with these 'inconvenient truths'.

Back to winding new bobbins. I handle them with extreme care, using a delicate touch responsive to each thread in turn, some as fine as hair. The pencil-slim bobbins I use are made of bone and wood, sometimes inscribed as love tokens ('Dear Hannah'), as tombstones ('Ann Brum, Radstone, 1840'), for the birth of a baby or even to commemorate a public hanging. It was by chance that I came across 'Joseph Castle, hung 1860'. Joseph, who murdered his wife Jane, was hanged in Luton and his in-laws held a memorial event at which participants were given commemorative bobbins. I have not used this one for decades but I hang it on my pillow with huge satisfaction, coming back to my roots in traditional lacemaking after long abandoning the fine traditional Bucks point and Bedfordshire laces for which the bobbin was made.

Bobbins are 'spangled', threaded on wire with beads. Everyone (even Queen Victoria when shown lacemaking at the Great Exhibition) asks the same thing: do these tell you which one to use? No, they just help to tension the thread, balance the bobbins in your hand and stop them rolling. A pretty pillow is part of the pleasure of lacemaking, for you do not look at the bobbins when you use them – your entire attention is focused on the work, on the twitch of the right thread as you lift it, and the way it weaves through the next.

The British artist David Hockney has talked of 'seeing with memory', where the significance of what appears today is sharpened by the image lingering in our minds from yesterday. Tension is the basis of lace construction, the pull and push of threads steadied by pins as work proceeds, woven and twisted to create figure and supporting ground. While old laces are underpinned by fixed geometric grids, nature's tensions stretch like chewing gum, a ballet of opposing forces that leaves ephemeral traces. It is those that have come to intrigue me in my attempts to capture the land as it burgeons, decays and transforms.

A journal of nature & story